SMOCKING
FOR PLEASURE

MADELINE BIRD·MARGIE PRESTEDGE

NEW
HOLLAND

To our children
Lynne, Leigh-Anne, Alasdair and Michaela
without whom we would never have
been inspired to smock

First published in the UK in 1989 by
New Holland (Publishers) Ltd
37 Connaught Street, London W2 2AZ

Reprinted in 1991

ISBN 1 85368 114 8 (hbk)
ISBN 1 85368 085 0 (pbk)

Editor: Anne Bryce
Designer: Poul-Ejnar Hansen
Cover design: Paul Wood
Illustrations: Gill Moorcroft
Phototypeset by Diatype Setting
Reproduction by Unifoto (Pty) Ltd
Printed and bound in Singapore by
Kyodo Printing Co (Singapore) Pte Ltd

Patterns for the garments that appear in this
book are available from: SMICKETY SMOCKS
                      P.O. BOX 138
                      NEWLANDS 7725
                      CAPE TOWN

                      FAX: 27 21 6834160

Contents

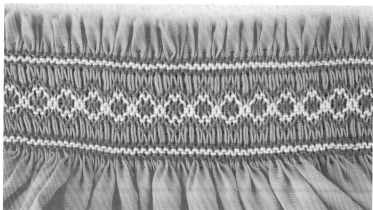

Fiona in a conventional yoke dress

Ian in a picture-smocked suit

Madeline Bird's love of smocking dates back to her childhood, when she wore beautifully smocked dresses made by her mother, an expert seamstress; having two daughters of her own inspired her to continue the tradition. Madeline has given smocking lessons for the past eight years and has contributed several articles on smocking to various women's magazines. She lives with her husband and two children.

Margie Prestedge became one of Madeline's pupils when friends convinced her that the baby she was expecting would be a little girl. A son arrived instead, but her interest in smocking had taken root. She and Madeline became close friends and their mutual love of smocking led to the decision to produce this book. Margie, who has recently begun giving lessons herself, lives with her husband, son and baby daughter.

Acknowledgements

It is impossible for us to express adequately our appreciation to all those who have made this book possible. However, special thanks go to our photographer, AAGE BUUS, *for his relentless patience and diligence,* GILL MOORCROFT *for her innovative illustrations, and* COLLEEN BOWERS *for the many hours she spent carefully assembling our garments and projects. At the same time, we would like to thank the many friends who so willingly loaned us their antiques and opened their beautiful homes to provide interesting backgrounds for the photographs, as well as the children who modelled our garments and their parents who helped in ways too numerous to mention.*

Our appreciation and thanks also go to:
LIZZIE O'HANLON, PENNY McADAM *and* SANDY JACOBS, *who efficiently transformed our longhand manuscript into acceptable typescript*

POUL-EJNAR HANSEN, *who designed this book, for his patience and for allowing us to become so involved in the design*

ANNE BRYCE, *for the many hours spent editing the manuscript*

J & P COATS (PTY) LTD, *for their continued interest and support*

LANDBOU WEEKBLAD *for permission to use the photograph on p. 28 and* SARIE *for permission to use the photograph on p. 72*

Finally, and most importantly, we wish to thank our husbands, MICHAEL *and* GORDON. *Without their sustained support, interest and constant encouragement, not only could this book never have been undertaken, but it could not have given us as much pleasure as it has.*

Introduction

Madeline and Margie's love of smocking, as well as the interest, encouragement and enthusiasm of families, friends and pupils, inspired the writing of this book. In the eight years during which Madeline has taught smocking, she has had numerous requests from far and near to write a guide which would help the beginner to grasp the fundamentals of smocking, as well as give experienced smockers useful hints and new ideas. The result is this comprehensive reference book for techniques from basic stitches to innovative garment construction.

Smocking, like patchwork, has been 'rediscovered' during the last few years and has grown in popularity worldwide. English smocking, a creative needlework form with much decorative charm, had its origins in Anglo-Saxon Britain. In those days, smocked garments were worn by men, always as outer garments. They were embroidered heavily on the sleeves and yoke with the design usually depicting the wearer's occupation. Over the centuries, the craft has spread throughout the world and today it is practised in countries as diverse as Spain, the Philippines, Hong Kong and the USA. It is only in the last 35 years, however, that the laborious and boring method of preparing the fabric for

smocking by hand has been automated with the advent of the smocking pleater – a marvellous machine which can put in as many as 32 gathering thread rows with the turn of a handle.

Smocking is far simpler than it appears, yet it allows plenty of scope for creative expression in terms of colour and design. Although few things look more attractive than a little girl in a smocked party dress, the craft is not limited to children's clothes, as this book illustrates.

In their aim of fulfilling the needs of both beginner and accomplished smocker, the authors have made extensive use of graphic drawings to illustrate the various stitches, and have included as large a variety of suggested designs as possible in the many colour photographs. The all-important (though often neglected) aspect of garment construction, and in particular incorporation of the smocked piece, has been dealt with fully.

Madeline and Margie have brought years of accumulated knowledge and a wealth of experience to this book, making it an invaluable guide to the fascinating craft of smocking.

Basic principles of smocking

Smocking is a very simple form of embroidery and yet is highly decorative. The endless combinations of stitches and patterns make it a versatile and satisfying needlework craft.

The embroidery stitches that are worked on top of the pleats serve to control their fullness, while retaining the elasticity which makes the garment comfortable to wear and practical to make. A child is able to wear a garment for longer because the smocking will continue to stretch. However, if it is stretched too far it will pucker.

Gathering thread rows are used as guidelines to hold the smocking stitches and keep the pleats in position during smocking.

The depth of the smocking stitches should be no more than halfway between the top of the pleat and the gathering thread row.

Generally, smocking is worked from left to right for right-handed smockers, the reverse being true if you are left-handed. Use a No. 7 crewel embroidery needle for all smocking projects.

Selecting fabric

When selecting fabric for smocking, take into consideration the colour, texture and washability of the material. Most important, the fabric should be of a good quality and should suit the colouring of the child. Many modern fabrics have a high nylon content, which is inclined to make the pleats 'pop out'. This makes smocking the piece more difficult. To eliminate this problem, use a spray-on starch on the wrong side of the fabric and iron the material before putting it through the smocking pleater (see p. 16).

When choosing fabric, bear in mind that plain fabrics will show up every smocked stitch, while small prints look very attractive on children. Any fabric that has a check, a stripe, or a stripe with a superimposed pattern is unsuitable for smocking a garment with a circular neck.

Fine fabrics draw up more tightly than heavier fabrics and therefore one must allow more material for the smocked area when selecting a finer weave. Broderie Anglaise with large holes is an unsuitable fabric for smocking as the stitches become distorted.

Most fabrics today are sold in widths of 115 cm (45 inches). A rule of thumb for calculating the amount of fabric required for a garment is to measure the length of the person from shoulders to hemline. Double this measurement, add the length of the sleeve and you will be able to gauge how much you need.

The smocked skirts of all children's dresses are 90 cm (36 inches) wide. Smocked skirts for adults are 115 cm (45 inches) wide and for babies, 76 cm (30 inches) wide.

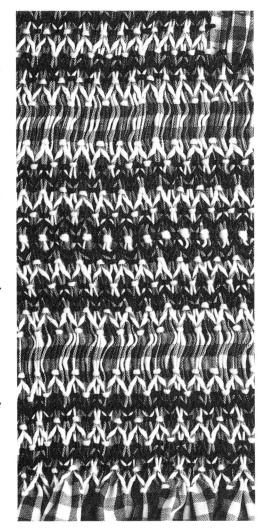

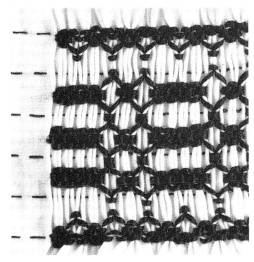

Opposite *Julia in a dress with a smocked bodice and Thomas in a playsuit with a smocked shirt*

Above *Detail of bodice*

Below *Detail of shirt*

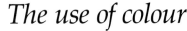

The use of colour

Colour is a vital part of this needle craft and it is important to make a study of how to use colour to achieve the effect you want.

Begin by working with colours you enjoy. One way to increase your colour consciousness is to mix different colours together until you create a pleasing effect.

The most important point to remember when working on your design is that your choice of colour must have the maximum effect on the background of the fabric, whether plain or patterned. The degree of contrast may be used with dramatic effect.

The colour grouping is usually more pleasing when a dominant colour is used with a lighter one. Use a single colour to achieve a focal effect and remember that repeating a colour throughout a design creates a certain harmony.

A useful and safe rule of thumb for the inexperienced smocker when choosing embroidery thread is to select a shade darker than the design in the fabric and a lighter one of the same colour tone. A contrast colour may be included to add interest and focus to the design.

An important point to remember is that orange and red are 'advancing' colours, because they have longer wavelengths, whereas blue and violet tend to recede. White and yellow are used for 'lifting' a design and show up well on dark fabrics. White may be used to highlight any area of a design.

Be wary of very shiny fabrics, as they reflect too much light and detract from the design.

It is interesting to note that by changing only one colour in a design the whole effect can be altered; this is one of the factors which makes smocking such an intriguing craft.

Planning your design

Work out your design before pleating the fabric. When designing smocks for infants, plan on using the fine spacing on a smocking pleater.

To centre a large design, first count the pleats to find the centre of the piece. Start the motif on the centre pleat and work towards the outer edge of the smocked piece. Each successive row of smocking must begin and end on the same pleat.

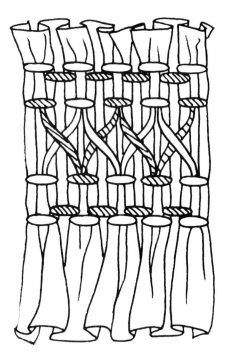

When smocking the back of a garment, leave six pleats on either side of the centre back marking, to allow for a placket or seam. This also ensures that each back section has the identical amount of smocking.

Selecting embroidery thread

Embroidery thread is available in a vast variety of colours. When selecting thread for your design it is a good idea to choose a shade that is darker rather than lighter than the shade of your fabric. Always write down the number of the colour selected.

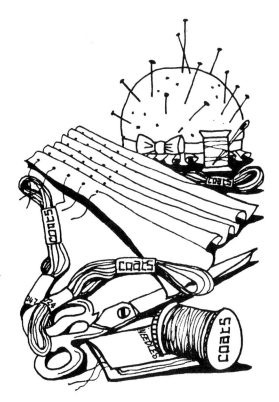

Most smocking stitches may be done with any number of strands of thread. The majority of the designs in this book have been worked with six strands of Coats Anchor stranded embroidery thread. In general, the number of strands you choose to work with depends on personal taste, the look you want to achieve and the weight of the fabric. For a finer fabric use fewer strands and for a heavier fabric up to six strands.

It is always advisable to 'strip' the embroidery thread, particularly when doing fill-in stitches and stacking of cable stitches. To do this, hold the piece of thread at one end between the thumb and forefinger. Separate the six strands and run a wet thumb and forefinger down each one. Referring to the end you are holding as the 'top', ensure that you keep all the 'top' ends together after stripping. Holding them together, select the number you require. Stripping will ensure a flat and uniform look to your work.

Calculate the length of embroidery thread needed for each row by measuring three times the gathered width of the piece to be smocked. Knot the thread at one end before starting a row of smocking.

Should you run out of thread in the middle of a row, push the needle to the back of your work through a 'valley'. End off by stitching two backstitches through the last pleat on the wrong side. To begin work again, knot a new piece of embroidery thread and come up in the same 'valley'.

Tension

It is very important to maintain a consistent tension when smocking so that your completed design looks neat. For correct tension, pull up the thread gently until you feel a slight resistance.

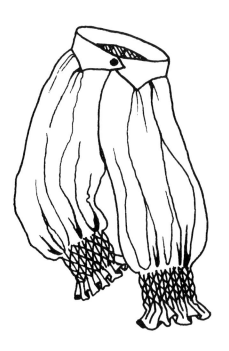

Stitches pulled too tightly will draw the pleats out of alignment, distorting them and causing the embroidery thread to lose its fullness and appear less visible. The elasticity of the completed piece of smocking will be reduced as well. (An over-worked design also has little elasticity.) Stitches that are too loose will not lie in position correctly and will make the work look untidy.

Pull the gathering threads out only once the smocking design has been completed.

As an approximate gauge, pull up the gathering threads so that the pleated area measures about 2,5 cm (1 inch) narrower than the piece to which it will be attached in the final garment construction.

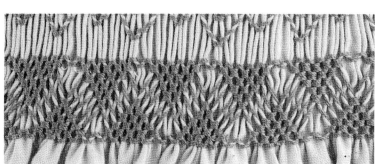

Samantha in an adult's peasant smock

14

Gathering the fabric

The preparation of fabric to be smocked is extremely important.
Several different methods may be used to gather the fabric into the
uniform, evenly pleated 'canvas' on which the smocking is done:

- *Smocking transfer dots*
- *Spotted fabric*
- *Checked fabric or gingham*
- *Smocking pleater*

Smocking transfer dots

Smocking transfer dots are available in several colours and
spacings. Select a transfer sheet with a smaller spacing of dots for a
fine fabric and a wider spacing for heavier fabric.

Cut a piece of transfer paper with the applicable number of rows of
dots, according to the smocking design that has been worked out
for your project. Before transferring the dots, pre-test your fabric to
ensure that the dots will not 'bleed through' the fabric to the right
side. If they do, they will be difficult to wash out.

Pin or tape the right side of this piece of transfer paper securely to
the wrong side of the fabric so that it will not move. Using the
lowest dry heat setting that will clearly transfer the dots to the
fabric, iron firmly over the transfer paper. Do this once only so as
not to smudge the dots.

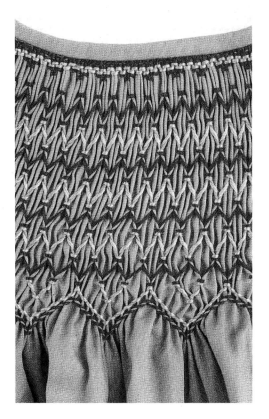

Above *Juliette in a raglan sleeve smocked dress*

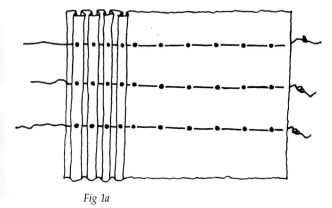

Fig 1a

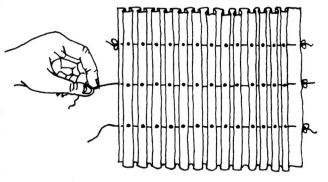

Fig 1b

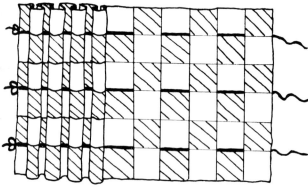

Fig 2a

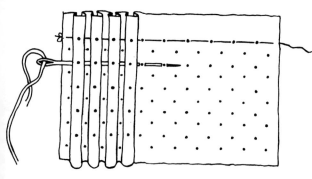

Fig 2b

Remove the transfer paper. Using a double thread of contrasting colour, pick up the dots, several at a time, working from right to left. Take care to ensure that the needle goes in one side of the dot and comes out on the other side of the same dot. Pick up each row of dots with a new thread. *(Fig 1a)*

Once all the rows of dots have been picked up, pull up these gathering thread rows, two rows at a time, until the pleated piece measures 2,5 cm (1 inch) narrower than the yoke to which it will be attached. Tie a knot at the end of each thread to prevent the pleats from pulling out. *(Fig 1b)*

To enable you to make perfect stitches in the first and last rows of your smocking design, add an extra gathering thread row above and below the gathering thread row on which you propose to start and finish your design.

Once the fabric has been prepared for smocking, pull the pleats straight from top to bottom and set them with steam.

Spotted and gingham (checked) fabric

Spotted or gingham fabrics provide their own guidelines. The weight of the fabric will determine the spacing of the pleats. Smaller pleats should be picked up on fine fabrics and larger pleats on heavier fabrics.

As in the instructions for picking up smocking dots, run gathering threads in a contrasting colour in rows across the fabric, using the check or spot in the fabric as your guide. *(Fig 2a & b)*

Once the fabric has been prepared for smocking, pull the pleats straight from top to bottom and set them with steam.

Smocking pleater

The laborious and boring method of preparing fabric for smocking by picking up transfer dots has been automated with the advent of the smocking pleater. In a fraction of the time it takes to prepare the fabric by hand, this wonderful gadget puts in as many as 32 gathering thread rows with just a turn of the handle. These smocking pleaters are available in three sizes – 16, 24 and 32. The size indicates the maximum number of gathering thread rows that can be drawn up at one time.

Place the smocking pleater on the table in front of you with the shafts of the needles facing you.

Starting from the left-hand side of the pleater, thread the number of needles required for your chosen design. Allow an extra gathering thread row at the top and bottom of the design and remember to allow for half spacings, if you intend to use these in your design.

For a 90 cm (36 inch) width of fabric, thread each of the required needles with 50 cm (20 inches) of thread of a contrasting colour to the fabric. Double the thread and knot the end.

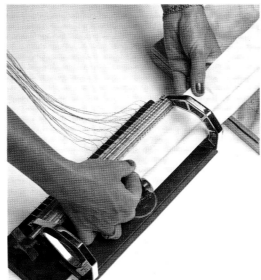
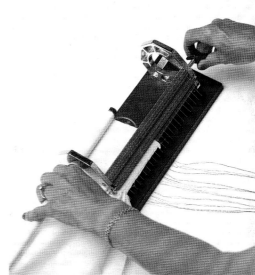

From left to right

1 *Threading the needles of the Sally Stanley 24-row pleater*

2 *Doubling the thread*

3 *Knotting the double thread*

4 *Rolling fabric onto dowel stick*

5 *Feeding fabric between back rollers*

6 *Turning handle of machine*

7 *Easing fabric onto thread*

8 *Cutting the thread*

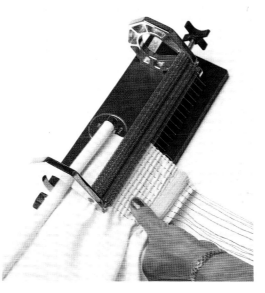

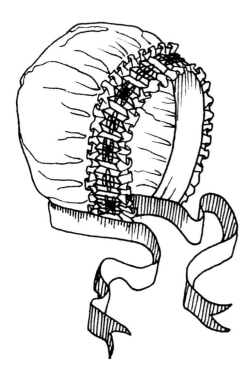

Cut the selvages off the fabric, but do not cut out the armholes or any other areas which will be cut away in the final construction of the garment. This is done only after the smocking has been completed.

With the top edge of the fabric on the left-hand side, roll the fabric onto a dowel stick, while rolling the dowel stick towards you.

Place the dowel stick with the fabric rolled onto it through the loops at the back of the pleater.

Ease the edge of the fabric between the two large rollers. Using your left hand to hold and steady the dowel stick, continue to feed the fabric evenly through the rollers, turning the handle with the right hand.

As the needles fill up with perfect pleats, ease the fabric gently onto the threads until the whole width of fabric is neatly and crisply pleated.

Cut the threads close to the eyes of the needles and tie them off to prevent the pleats from pulling out.

The preparation of the fabric for smocking is now complete, the machine having automatically gauged the size of the pleat according to the weight of the fabric.

To save re-threading the needles, two or more pieces of fabric, depending on their width, may be pleated on the same thread.

If your design requires more than the maximum number of gathering thread rows that your machine can provide, simply feed the fabric through the pleater twice. Feed it through the first time to pick up the excess rows which your pleater cannot accommodate. Leave the gathering threads the same length as the width of the material, so that the pleats can be pulled out and the fabric made to lie flat. Re-thread all the needles of the pleater except the last two on the right-hand side. Feed the fabric through a second time, keeping the last needle on the right-hand side going over the bottom gathering thread row of the section already pleated.

Pull up all the rows into tight pleats and run a gathering thread row between the two pleated areas by hand, to align the pleats.

It is not necessary to set the pleats with steam if a smocking pleater has been used.

When working on a sundress with a frill at the upper edge, remember to make a rolled hem on the frill edge before putting the fabric through the pleater. Keep the finished frill edge outside the left-hand side of the machine when feeding the fabric through.

Starting and ending

To start a row of smocking, knot one end of the embroidery thread, come up from the back of your work on the left-hand side of the pleat (a needle's width above the gathering thread row) and take a stitch through the next pleat, keeping the needle parallel to the gathering thread row.

To end a row, push the needle through to the back of your work on the right-hand side of the last pleat. Secure with two backstitches on top of the back of this pleat, or make a loop and knot.

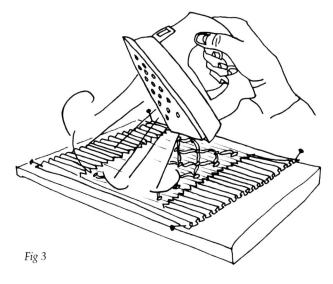

Fig 3

Blocking

Blocking is done by pinning the completed smocked piece to an ironing board and stretching it gently to fit the yoke to which it will be attached. Hold a hot steam iron above the smocked piece, being careful not to touch the smocking with the iron. While the smocked piece is still damp and pinned to the ironing board, pull the pleats into shape from top to bottom. *(Fig 3)*

An alternative to using steam to set the pleats is to spray the smocked piece with water while it is still attached to the ironing board and then to leave it to dry overnight.

Blocking of circular neck garments is dealt with on p. 83.

Picture smocking

Ideas gleaned from nursery rhymes or stories might inspire you to create a picture smock showing a colourful scene.

In picture smocking, the pleats are drawn up very tightly and the completed smocked piece is not stretched at all as this will distort the figures in the scene. For this reason, extra fabric should be allowed.

Draw the picture on graph paper or on the pleated fabric with a dressmaking pen. Strip the embroidery cotton and using 3 to 4 strands, fill in the areas of the picture that require colour, using cable, outline or trellis stitches. Backsmock any areas where there are more than 4 pleats that are unsmocked on the front.

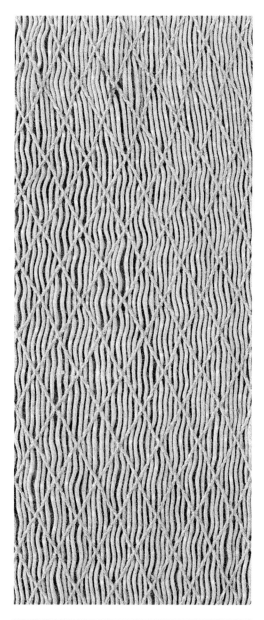

Backsmocking

Backsmocking is worked on the wrong side of the fabric to keep the pleats in position while free form or picture smocking is done on the front of the fabric. It is also used to hold pleats in position where there is to be no smocking in areas of a design.

Backsmocking is always done with thread of the same colour as the fabric, using only two strands. It is started and finished off on the same side as the backsmocking. Outline or cable stitch gives the appearance of straight rows on the right side, while trellis stitches create the effect of waves or diamonds.

Backsmocking is also used to balance the tension on both sides of the fabric, so that a ruffled neck edge will stand up straight rather than roll forward. In addition, it will give added support and strength around a cuff or the top of a sundress.

Hints and pitfalls

The following hints should prove useful to beginners in particular:

Fabric is heavier when smocked, due to the gathering.

When pleats 'pop out' it makes smocking very difficult. To eliminate this problem, use a spray-on starch on the wrong side of the fabric and iron the fabric before putting it through the smocking pleater.

When selecting embroidery thread, always write down the number of the chosen colour in case you have to buy another skein.

Mistakes may be corrected by using the eye end of the needle to pull out the incorrect stitches. Be careful not to split the cotton while doing so.

At the centre back of a garment, six pleats are left unsmocked to allow for a placket (a strip of fabric used to bind the raw edges of a slit cut in a garment to facilitate putting it on and taking it off).

Avoid cutting into smocking as it will unravel. However, should it be necessary to cut into a smocked piece, always stay stitch first along the edge to be cut.

After washing a garment, pull the pleats firmly back into place while the garment is still damp. The smocked areas are never ironed.

Loops of embroidery thread should not cross more than four pleats. It is preferable to end off and start afresh.

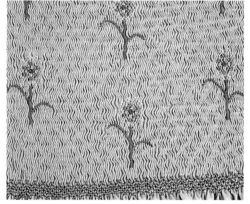

Opposite *Helen in a back-smocked dress*

Above *Details of backsmocking and front of bodice*

Basic stitch glossary

General rules for stitches

The following rules apply to most of the smocking stitches explained in this glossary:

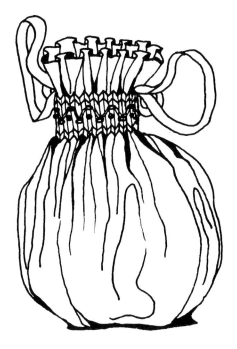

1. Always begin from the back of your work, a needle's width above the gathering thread row (unless otherwise stated).

2. The needle should always be kept parallel to the gathering thread.

3. The needle passes through one pleat at a time and should pick up the pleat as near the crest as possible. Avoid picking it up below the upper third of the pleat.

4. Use the needle as a tool to straighten and help position the stitches.

5. After pulling the needle and thread through the pleat, allow the stitch to settle on the pleat and give the thread a gentle tug.

6. Stitches are worked from left to right across the smocking for a right-handed person, and from right to left for a left-hander. If you are left-handed, turn this book upside down when following the diagrams of the smocking stitches.

7. For correct tension, pull up the thread gently until you feel a slight resistance. Stitches which are tugged too tightly will pull the pleats out of alignment, distorting them and causing the embroidery thread to lose its fullness and appear less visible. Stitches that are too loose will not lie in position correctly and will make the work look untidy.

8. Be prepared to spend a little time at the beginning, checking the first row of stitches for mistakes and removing incorrect stitches with the eye end of the needle. If a mistake is not corrected in the first row, it should be repeated in all other rows to retain the design.

9. Most smocking stitches may be done with any number of strands of thread. However, there are a few which cannot be done with six strands, which is the number used for most smocking designs in this book. On the whole, the number of strands you choose to work with depends on personal taste, the look you want to achieve and the weight of the fabric.

10. Never begin a smocking stitch on the first pleat of a smocking piece, but rather on the third or fifth pleat. This leaves sufficient space for a reasonably sized seam on either side of the smocked piece when you incorporate it into your project.

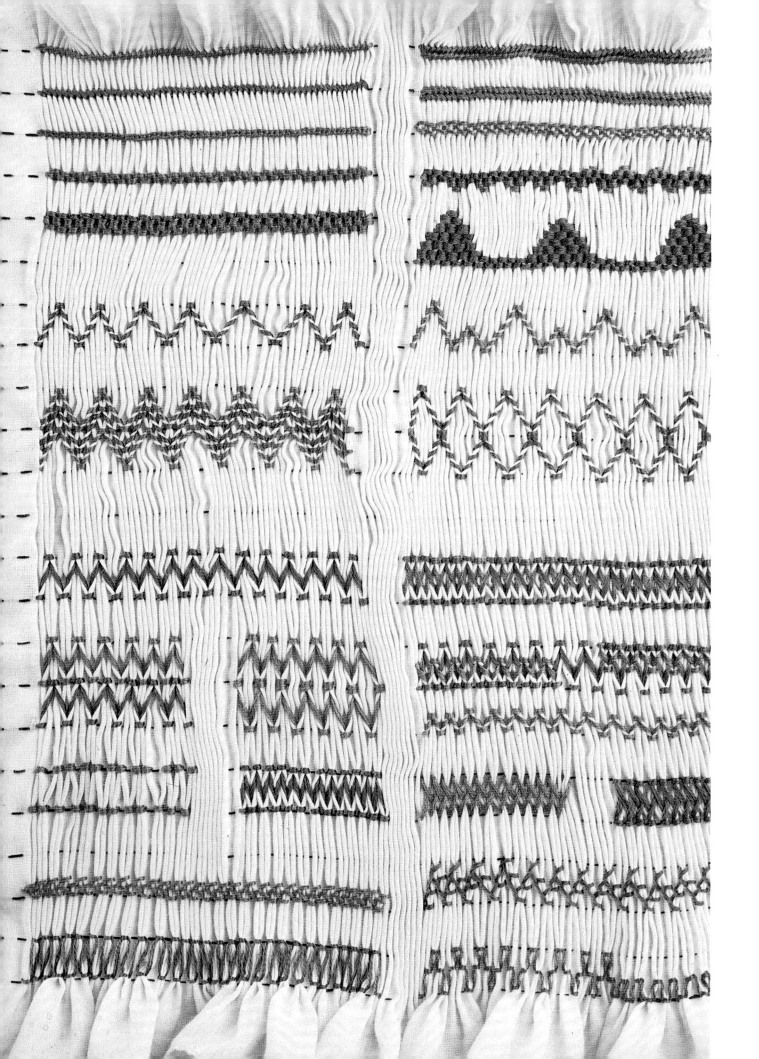

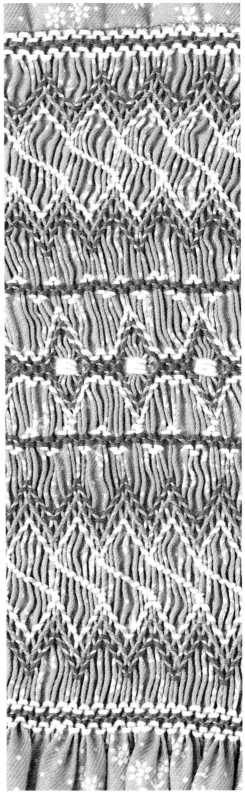

Opposite *Basic stitch sampler*

Left *Emma in a conventional yoke dress smocked to the waist*

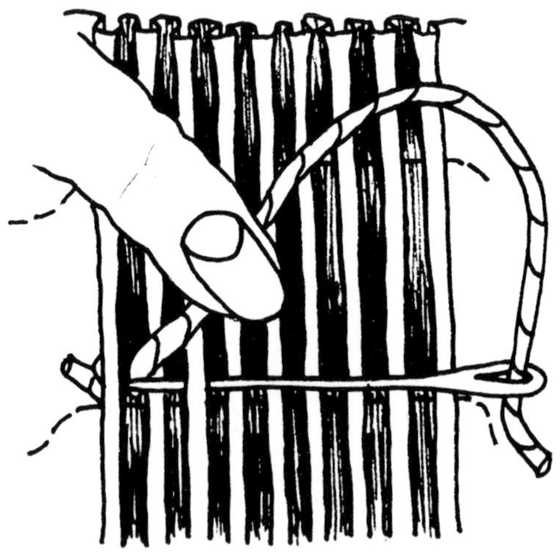

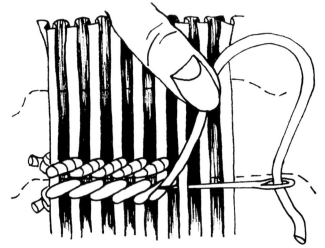

Fig 4a

Fig 4b

Fig 4c

Straight stitches

This set of stitches is fairly non-elastic and therefore helps to control the fullness of the fabric – for example around the cuff of a blouse or in the first group of stitches around a circular neck. Straight stitches are the most commonly used in backsmocking, in which the rows of stitches are worked on the back of the fabric to hold the pleats in position, while free form smocking is done on the front of the fabric. Generally, these stitches are worked straight across the pleats, following the gathering thread and thus helping to keep the work straight. They may, however, be 'stacked' as in picture smocking or curved to form shapes in free form smocking designs.

There are five basic straight stitches:

- *Outline stitch*
- *Stem stitch*
- *Chain stitch*
- *Raised chain stitch*
- *Cable stitch*

Outline stitch

When doing this stitch, the thread should always be above the needle. The stitch is worked from left to right.

1. Come up from the back of your work (a needle's width above the gathering thread row) on the left-hand side of the 3rd pleat. (*Fig 4a*)

2. With the thread above the needle, pick up the next pleat at the same level on the right-hand side of the pleat and come out on the left-hand side.

3. Pull the needle and thread through the pleat and as the stitch settles on the pleat, give the thread a gentle downward tug before putting the thread above the needle and proceeding to pick up the next pleat. (*Fig 4b*)

4. Pick up the next pleat at the same level and depth as the previous one.

Variation

Smock a second and possibly even a third row one beneath the other (*Fig 4c*), as shown in the photographed sampler on p. 24.

Stem stitch

Stem stitch is worked in exactly the same way as outline stitch, except that the thread is always below the needle. In this case, when you pull the needle and thread through the pleat, as the stitch settles on the pleat, give the thread a gentle upward tug before putting the thread below the needle again. This stitch is worked from left to right, putting the thread below the needle before proceeding to pick up the next pleat. (*Fig 5a & b*)

Variation

This basic stitch, as with outline stitch, may be varied by smocking a second and possibly a third row one beneath the other (*Fig 5c*), as shown on p. 24.

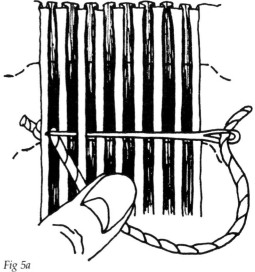

Fig 5a

Fig 5b

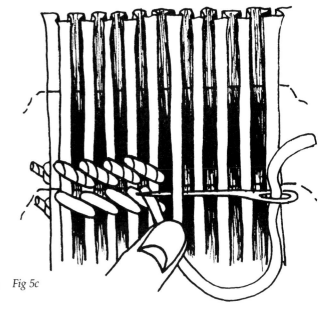

Fig 5c

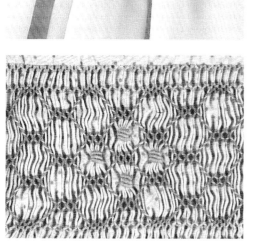

Above right *Justin in a smocked romper*

Below *Lynne and Leigh-Anne in smocked nightdresses*

Opposite *Caroline in a smocked nightdress*

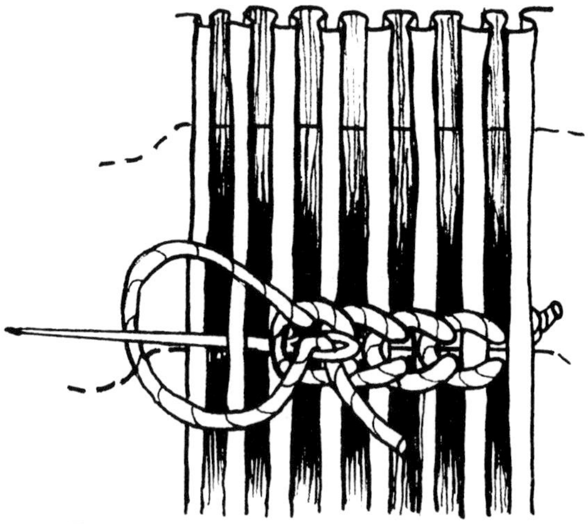

Chain stitch

The chain stitch may be worked across the gathering thread row or worked into curves to outline and form various shapes. It is a very tight stitch with almost no stretch. Use 3 or 4 strands of embroidery thread for this stitch, which is worked from right to left.

1. Come up from the back of your work (on the gathering thread row), on the right-hand side of the 3rd pleat.

2. With the thread below the needle, pick up the next pleat at the same level on the left-hand side of the pleat and come out on the right-hand side.

3. Pull the needle and thread through the pleat to form a large loop. Continue to draw the thread through to form a smaller loop that sits neatly on the pleat.

4. Insert the needle on the gathering thread row through the loop and then through the next pleat, keeping the thread below the needle.

5. Continue working your chain stitch across the pleats in this way. *(Fig 6)*

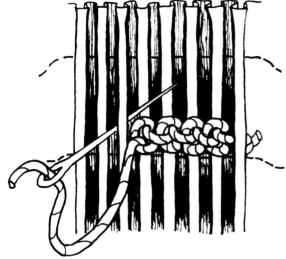

Fig 6

Raised chain stitch

The raised chain stitch is similar to ordinary chain stitch, but the needle is inserted into the same pleat twice. It is a very tight stitch with almost no stretch. Use 3 or 4 strands of embroidery thread. The stitch is worked from right to left.

1. Come up from the back of your work (on the gathering thread row) on the right-hand side of the 3rd pleat.

2. With the thread below the needle and the needle slanting up to the right, pick up the next pleat a needle's width above the gathering thread row. *(Fig 7a)*

3. Pull the needle and thread through the pleat.

4. Make a large loop to the left. With the thread below the needle and the needle slanting up to the left, pick up the same pleat a needle's width below the gathering thread row. Pull the needle and thread through the pleat to form a large loop. Continue to draw the thread into a small loop that sits neatly on the pleat. *(Fig 7b)*

5. With the thread below the needle and the needle slanting up to the right, pick up the next pleat a needle's width above the gathering thread row.

6. Pull the needle and thread through the pleat.

7. Continue working the raised chain stitch across the pleats in this way.

Fig 7a

Fig 7b

Cable stitch

The thread is alternated above and below the needle on successive pleats. Always begin a row of cable stitch with a 'bottom' cable. For a 'top' cable the thread is above the needle and for a 'bottom' cable it is below the needle. This stitch is worked from left to right.

1. Come up from the back of your work (a needle's width above the gathering thread row), on the left-hand side of the 3rd pleat.

2. With the thread below the needle, pick up the next pleat at the same level on the right-hand side of the pleat and come out on the left-hand side. *(Fig 8a)*

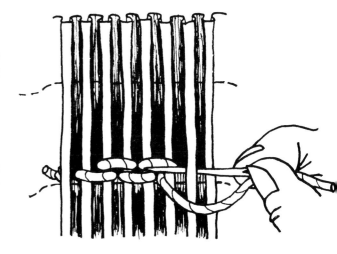

Fig 8a

3. Pull the needle and thread through the pleat and give the thread a gentle upward tug before putting the thread above the needle and proceeding to pick up the next pleat. You have now made a 'bottom' cable.

4. With the thread above the needle, pick up the next pleat at the same level on the right-hand side of the pleat and come out on the left-hand side. *(Fig 8b)*

5. Pull the needle and thread through the pleat and give the thread a gentle downward tug before putting the thread below the needle and proceeding to pick up the next pleat. You have now made a 'top' cable.

6. Continue to work across successive pleats in this way, alternating the thread above and below the needle.

Variations

Cable stitches may be combined in various ways (*Fig 8c*) to produce many interesting designs, as shown on p. 24.

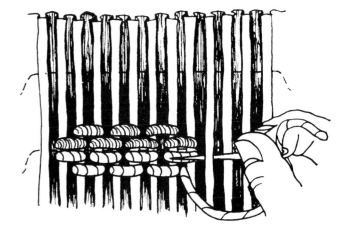

Fig 8b

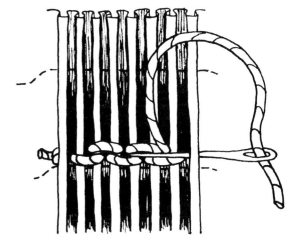

Fig 8c

Fig 9a

Fig 9b

Fig 9c

Zigzag stitches

This set of stitches is very versatile and has much more elasticity than the straight stitches. This group is worked between gathering thread rows.

The following are useful rules to apply when doing zigzag stitches:

When going up, keep the thread down i.e. when going up the zigzag, keep the thread below the needle.

When going down, keep the thread up i.e. when going down the zigzag, keep the thread above the needle.

Keep the thread above the needle for a top cable and below the needle for a bottom cable.

There are six basic zigzag stitches:

- *Trellis or waves*
- *Chevron*
- *Honeycomb*
- *Herringbone*
- *Feather*
- *Van Dyke*

Trellis or waves

A wave or trellis always starts and ends with a bar or cable stitch. The spacing of the stitches going up the wave from the bottom to the top positions between two rows of gathering threads may be varied. However, the most popularly used spacings are ¼, ⅓ and ½ spacings with 4, 3 and 2 steps respectively between the bar stitch on one gathering thread row and the bar stitch on the adjacent row.

A wave or trellis may be built to various heights. Waves are all worked from left to right.

Full space

1. Come up from the back of your work (a needle's width above the 2nd gathering thread row) on the left-hand side of the 3rd pleat.

2. With the thread below the needle, pick up the next pleat at the same level on the right-hand side of the pleat and come out on the left-hand side.

3. Pull the needle and thread through the pleat and as the stitch settles on the pleat, give the thread a gentle upward tug before putting the thread down again to go up the wave.

4. Use the needle to straighten and help position the 'bottom' bar stitch you have just made. Progress up the wave to the gathering thread row on the line above. For convenience, we shall illustrate a 3-step wave.

5. With the thread below the needle, pick up the next pleat ⅓ of the distance between the gathering thread rows on the right-hand side of the pleat and come out on the left-hand side.

6. Pull needle and thread through the pleat and give the thread a gentle upward tug before putting it below the needle again.

32

7. Continue by positioning each new stitch on a successive pleat, taking an additional ⅓ of the space each time.

8. When the wave reaches the next gathering thread row, make a 'top' bar. With the thread above the needle, pick up the next pleat.

9. Pull the needle and thread through the pleat and give the thread a gentle downward tug before putting the thread above the needle to come down the wave, using the same space intervals as when you went up.

10. At the bottom of the completed wave make a 'bottom' bar again as previously described. (Fig 9a)

Half space

This stitch is worked in the same way as the full space wave but is only worked to the halfway point between the two gathering thread rows. (Fig 9b)

Variations

Any number of rows of waves may be repeated one beneath the other at various intervals, as shown on p. 24. However, the larger the number of rows, the tighter the smocked area becomes. (Fig 9c)

Diamonds

To form diamonds, two rows of waves are worked opposite each other. Work one row as previously described and once completed, work the opposite row. Where the bottom bar of the first row of waves meets the top bar of the opposite row, slide the needle up between the pleats and insert in the same hole used to make the bottom bar of the first row of waves, taking care not to cover the bottom bar stitches of this row. This will ensure that the diamonds are symmetrical from top to bottom. (Fig 9d)

Variations

Any number of rows of waves may be repeated on either side of the diamond to form a most effective variation.

You could also work a row of diamonds, one below the other, as another variation.

Waves of different sizes in the same row

This is a line of waves of varying heights repeated systematically throughout a row. (Fig 9e)

Variations

Any number of rows may be repeated one below the other at various intervals.

Two rows of waves of varying heights may be worked opposite each other to form diamonds.

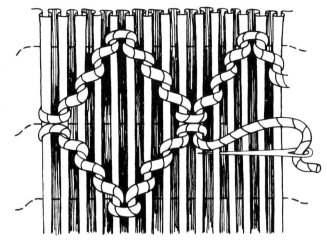

Fig 9d

Fig 9e

Lynne in a blouse with a smocked square yoke

34

Fiona in a christening dress with a conventional yoke

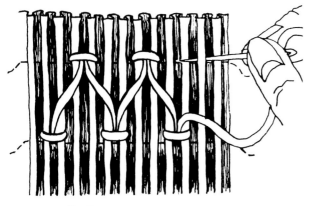

Fig 10a

Chevron

This stitch is sometimes referred to as a 'one step wave' or a 'baby wave' and may be worked over a full or half space. A chevron starts and ends with a bar or cable stitch and is worked from left to right.

Full space and half space

1. Come up from the back of your work (a needle's width above the 2nd gathering thread row) on the left of the 3rd pleat.

2. With the thread below the needle, pick up the next pleat at the same level on the right-hand side of the pleat and come out on the left-hand side.

3. Pull the needle and thread through the pleat and as the stitch settles on the pleat, give the thread a gentle upward tug before putting the thread down again to go to the 'up' point.

4. With the thread below the needle, pick up the next pleat at the 'up' point, which may be a needle's width above the next gathering thread row (i.e. a full space above), or a needle's width above the halfway point between the gathering thread rows (i.e. a half space) on the right-hand side of the pleat, and come out on the left-hand side of that pleat.

5. Pull the needle and thread through the pleat and as the stitch settles on the pleat, give the thread a gentle upward tug, taking care not to pull the thread too tightly as the pleats will distort very easily when doing a chevron stitch.

6. Now make a top bar. With the thread above the needle, pick up the next pleat at the same level as your last stitch, on the right-hand side of the pleat and come out on the left-hand side.

7. Pull the needle and thread through the pleat and give the thread a gentle downward tug before putting it above the needle, in order to come down again to the gathering thread row on which you started.

8. With the thread above the needle, pick up the next pleat at the same level as the first bar stitch, pushing aside the two pleats you have already stitched. The pleat is picked up by the needle on the right-hand side of the pleat and comes out on the left-hand side.

9. Pull the needle and thread through the pleat and give the thread a gentle downward tug, taking care not to pull it too tightly.

10. With the thread below the needle, make a bottom bar stitch as previously described. *(Fig 10a)*

Chevron diamonds

To form chevron diamonds, two rows of chevron stitches are worked opposite each other. Work one row of chevron stitches as previously described and once completed, work the opposite row. Where the bottom bar of the first row of the chevron meets the top bar of the opposite row, slide the needle up between the pleats and

36

insert in the same hole used to make the bottom bar of the first row of the chevron, taking care not to cover the bottom bar stitches of this row.

This will ensure that the diamonds are symmetrical from top to bottom. A chevron diamond should always have two pleats in the centre of the diamond, as shown on p. 24. *(Fig 10b)*

Variations

Rows of diamonds may be worked above and below each other on either side of the diamond.

Any number of rows may be repeated one above or below the other, on either side of the diamond.

Chevrons and chevron diamonds of full and half space may be repeated systematically throughout a row.

Crossover chevrons

Work one row of full or half space chevron stitches, starting as always with a bottom bar. Over the top of this row work another row of chevron stitches − either full or half space − starting with a top bar stitch.

This variation of the basic chevron stitch is very effective when worked in two different colours *(Fig 10c)*, as shown on p. 24.

A useful rule of thumb when doing a crossover chevron is to use the darker or more dominant colour first and to work the lighter or less dominant colour over the top.

Special care should be taken not to pull the thread too tightly, as the chevron stitch is inclined to distort the pleats very easily.

Fig 10b

Fig 10c

Above right *Jenny with a smocked broderie Anglaise collar*

Below *Michaela in a smocked babygro*

Opposite *Alasdair in a smocked suit*

Honeycomb

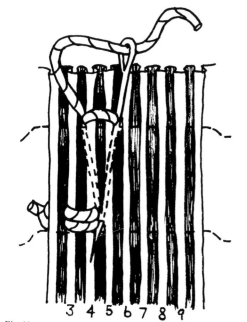

Fig 11a

Honeycomb is one of the most elastic smocking stitches and therefore does not need much fabric. In general, allow 7,5 cm (3 inches) of fabric to give 2,5 cm (1 inch) of finished smocking. This stitch is worked from left to right with embroidery thread of the same colour as the fabric so as not to be visible through the pleats. Do not use more than 3 strands of thread. Several rows of honeycomb should be done to achieve the diamond look created by this stitch. Start on alternate rows for the pattern to develop.

1. Come up from the back of your work (a needle's width above the 2nd gathering thread row) on the left of the 3rd pleat.

2. With the thread below the needle, pick up the next pleat (No. 4) at the same level on the right-hand side of the pleat and come out on the left-hand side of pleat No. 3. In this way you are inserting the needle through two pleats, thus coming out where you started.

3. Pull the needle and thread through the pleats and give the thread a gentle upward tug.

4. With the thread still below the needle, re-insert the needle into the same hole as where No. 4 pleat was entered, but point the needle up so that it travels up the back of the pleat and comes out just above the gathering thread of the row above.

5. Bring the needle up from the back of your work, on the left-hand side of the 4th pleat.

6. With the thread below the needle, pick up the next pleat (No. 5) at the same level on the right-hand side of the pleat and come out on the left-hand side of pleat No. 4. In this way you are inserting the needle through two pleats – No. 5 then No. 4.

7. Pull the needle and thread through the pleats.

8. With the thread above the needle, re-insert the needle into the same hole as where No. 5 pleat was entered, but point the needle down so that it travels down the back of the pleat and comes out just above the gathering thread of the row on which you started.

9. Bring the needle up from the back of your work, in the valley on the left-hand side of the 5th pleat.

10. With the thread below the needle, pick up the next pleat (No. 6) at the same level on the right-hand side of the pleat and come out on the left-hand side of pleat No. 5. In this way you are inserting the needle through two pleats – No. 6 then No. 5.

11. Pull the needle and thread through the pleats and give the thread a gentle upward tug.

12. With the thread still below the needle, re-insert the needle into the same hole as where No. 6 pleat was entered, but point the needle up so that it travels up the back of the pleat and comes out just above the gathering thread of the row above.

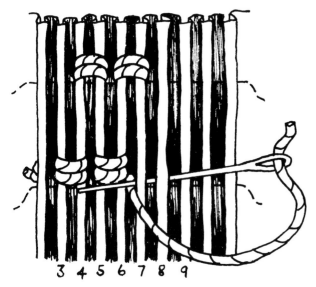

Fig 11b

13. Continue the row of honeycomb in this manner. (Fig 11a and 11b)

40

Surface honeycomb

Surface honeycomb is similar to the chevron stitch but two stitches are made into the same pleat, i.e. you remain on the same pleat when you move up or down and pick up a new pleat only when making a top or bottom bar. Surface honeycomb begins and ends with a bar or cable stitch. This stitch is worked from left to right.

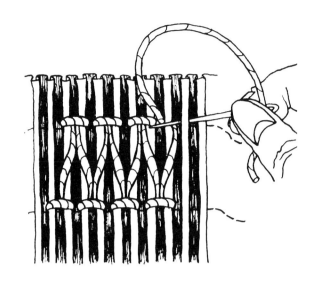

Fig 12

1. Come up from the back of your work (a needle's width above the 2nd gathering thread row), on the left of the 3rd pleat.

2. With the thread below the needle, pick up the next pleat (No. 4) at the same level on the right-hand side of the pleat and come out on the left-hand side.

3. Pull the needle through the pleat and give the thread a gentle upward tug, before putting it down again to go to the 'up' point.

4. With the thread below the needle, pick up the same pleat (No. 4) at the 'up' point, which may be a needle's width above the next gathering thread row, or a needle's width above the halfway point between the gathering thread rows on the right-hand side of the pleat, and come out on the left-hand side.

5. Pull the needle and thread through the pleat and give the thread a gentle upward tug, taking care not to pull too tightly, as the pleats will distort very easily.

6. Now make a top bar. With the thread above the needle, pick up the next pleat (No. 5) at the same level as your last stitch on the right-hand side of the pleat and come out on the left-hand side.

7. Pull the needle and thread through the pleat and give the thread a gentle downward tug, before putting the thread above the needle and coming down again to the 2nd gathering thread row.

8. With the thread above the needle, pick up the same pleat (No. 5) at the same level as the first bar stitch on the right-hand side of the pleat and come out on the left-hand side.

9. Pull the needle and thread through the pleat and give the thread a gentle downward tug, taking care not to pull too tightly.

10. With the thread below the needle, pick up the next pleat (No. 6) to make a bottom bar stitch as described above. *(Fig 12)*

Honeycomb diamond

To form diamonds, two rows of surface honeycomb are worked opposite each other. Work one row of surface honeycomb as previously described and once completed, work the opposite row. Where the bottom bar of the first row of surface honeycomb meets the top bar of the opposite row, slide the needle up between the pleats and insert it in the same hole used to make the bottom bar of the first row of surface honeycomb. Take care not to cover the bottom bar stitches of this row. This will ensure that the diamonds are symmetrical from top to bottom. There are no pleats in the centre of a honeycomb diamond, whereas there are two pleats in the centre of each chevron diamond.

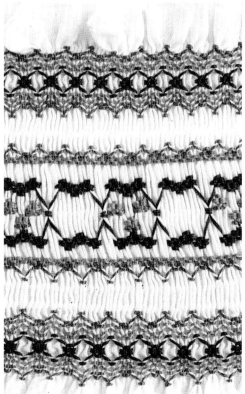

Right *Emma in a smocked pinafore with a square neck*

Opposite *Susan in a pinafore smocked to the waist*

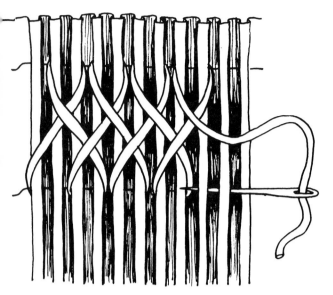

Fig 13a

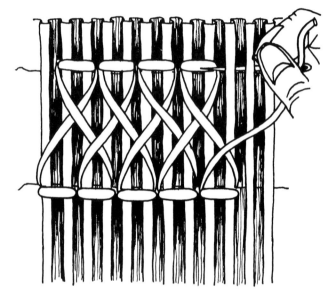

Fig 13b

Herringbone

Herringbone stitch does not have any bar stitches at its top and bottom positions. The needle is passed through two pleats at once (an old pleat and a new one). The stitch is worked from left to right.

1. Come up from the back of your work (on the 2nd gathering thread row) on the left-hand side of the 3rd pleat.

2. With the thread below the needle, pick up pleat No. 5 a needle's width above the first gathering thread row on the right-hand side, and come out on the left-hand side of pleat No. 4. In this way you are inserting the needle through two pleats – No. 5 then No. 4.

3. Pull the needle and thread through the pleats.

4. With the thread above the needle, pick up pleat No. 6 a needle's width above the 2nd gathering thread row and come out on the left-hand side of pleat No. 5.

5. Pull the needle and thread through the pleats.

6. With the thread below the needle, pick up pleat No. 7, then No. 6 at the 'up' point and continue to work across the row in this way. *(Fig 13a)*

Double herringbone

Double herringbone is similar to herringbone stitch except that it has a bar stitch at the top and bottom positions. It is a tighter stitch than herringbone and is therefore not as elastic. It is worked from left to right.

To do the bar stitch at the top and bottom positions, return to the right-hand side of the pleat and re-insert the needle into the same hole as the last stitch. Pull the needle and thread through the pleat and give the thread a gentle upward tug for a bottom bar and a downward tug for a top bar. *(Fig 13b)*

Feather stitch

Use 3 or 4 strands of embroidery cotton for this stitch. It is a fairly tight stitch with little stretch and is worked from right to left.

1. Come up from the back of your work (a needle's width below the gathering thread row), on the right-hand side of the 3rd pleat.

2. With the thread above the needle and slanting the needle at a 45° angle up to the left, pick up pleat No. 3 and No. 4, a needle's width below the gathering thread row.

3. Wrap the thread around the needle, forming a loop that runs from above to below the needle, on the left of the needle.

4. Pull the needle and thread through the loop.

5. With the thread below the needle and slanting the needle at a 45° angle down to the left, pick up pleat No. 4 and No. 5, a needle's width above the gathering thread row.

6. Wrap the thread around the needle, forming a loop that runs from below to above the needle, on the left of the needle.

7. Pull the needle and thread through the loop.

8. With the thread above the needle and slanting the needle at a 45° angle up to the left, pick up pleat No. 5 and No. 6 a needle's width below the gathering thread row.

9. Continue to work the feather stitch across the pleats in this way. (Fig 14a)

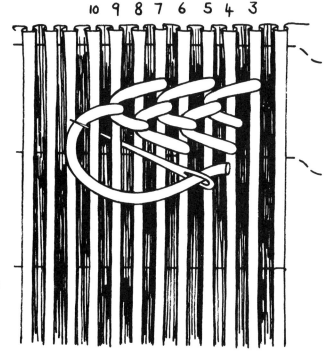

Fig 14a

Zigzag feather stitch

This is a variation of straight feather stitch.

1. Come up from the back of your work (a needle's width below the 2nd gathering thread row) on the right-hand side of the 3rd pleat.

2. With the thread above the needle, pick up pleat No. 3 a needle's width above the 2nd gathering thread row on the right-hand side, and come out on the left-hand side of pleat No. 4.

3. Wrap the thread around the needle forming a loop that runs from above to below on the left of the needle. Pull the needle and thread through the loop.

4. With the thread below the needle, pick up pleat No. 4 a needle's width above the halfway point between the gathering thread rows, on the right-hand side of the pleat, and come out on the left-hand side of pleat No. 5.

5. Wrap the thread around the needle, forming a loop that runs from below to above the needle on the left of the needle. Pull the needle and thread through the loop.

6. With the thread below the needle, pick up pleat No. 5 a needle's width above the next gathering thread row on the right-hand side of the pleat, and come out on the left-hand side of pleat No. 6.

Fig 14b

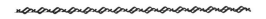

7. Wrap the thread around the needle forming a loop that runs from below to above on the left of the needle. Pull the needle and thread through the loop.

8. With the thread above the needle, pick up pleat No. 6 a needle's width above the halfway point between the gathering thread rows, on the right-hand side of the pleat, and come out on the left-hand side of pleat No. 7.

9. Wrap the thread around the needle forming a loop that runs from above to below on the left of the needle. Pull the needle and thread through the loop.

10. With the thread above the needle, pick up pleat No. 7 a needle's width above the gathering thread row on which you started, on the right-hand side of the pleat, and come out on the left-hand side of pleat No. 8.

11. Wrap the thread around the needle, forming a loop that runs from above to below the needle on the left of the needle. Pull the needle and thread through the loop.

12. Put the thread below the needle to go up the zigzag again. Continue working across the pleats in this way. *(Fig 14b)*

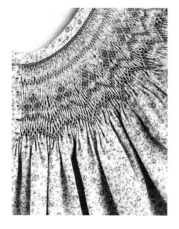

Opposite *Crib and lampshade smocking projects*

Above *Robyn and Victoria in smocked circular necked dresses with butterfly frills*

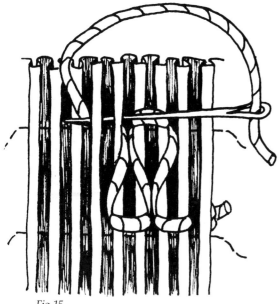

Fig 15

Van Dyke

Van Dyke stitch may be worked over a full or half space interval. It is a very tight stitch and therefore does not have much 'give'. The stitch is worked from right to left.

1.   Come up from the back of your work (a needle's width above the 2nd gathering thread row), on the right-hand side of the 3rd pleat.

2.   With the thread above the needle, pick up pleat No. 3 at the same level, on the right-hand side of the pleat, and come out on the left-hand side of pleat No. 4, so inserting the needle through two pleats. Pull the needle and thread through the pleats.

3.   With the thread still above the needle, return to the right-hand side of pleat No. 3 and re-insert the needle in the same hole as the last stitch, coming out again on the left-hand side of pleat No. 4.

4.   Pull the needle and thread through the pleats and give the thread a gentle downward tug.

5.   With the thread below the needle, pick up pleat No. 4 at the 'up' point, which may be a needle's width above the next gathering thread row (i.e. a full space above) or a needle's width above the halfway point between the gathering thread rows, on the right-hand side of the pleat, and come out on the left of pleat No. 5.

6.   Pull the needle and thread through the pleats.

7.   With the thread below the needle, return to the right-hand side of pleat No. 4 and re-insert the needle in the same hole as the last stitch, coming out again on the left-hand side of pleat No. 5.

8.   Pull the needle and thread through the pleats and give the thread a gentle upward tug.

9.   With the thread above the needle, pick up pleat No. 5 a needle's width above the gathering thread row on which you started, on the right-hand side of the pleat, and come out on the left-hand side of pleat No. 6. In this way you are inserting the needle through two pleats – No. 5 then No. 6.

10.   Pull the needle and thread through the pleats.

11.   With the thread above the needle, return to the right-hand side of pleat No. 5 and re-insert the needle in the same hole as the last stitch, coming out again on the left-hand side of pleat No. 5.

12.   Pull the needle and thread through the pleats and continue to work across the row in this way. *(Fig 15)*

Opposite *Combination stitch sampler*

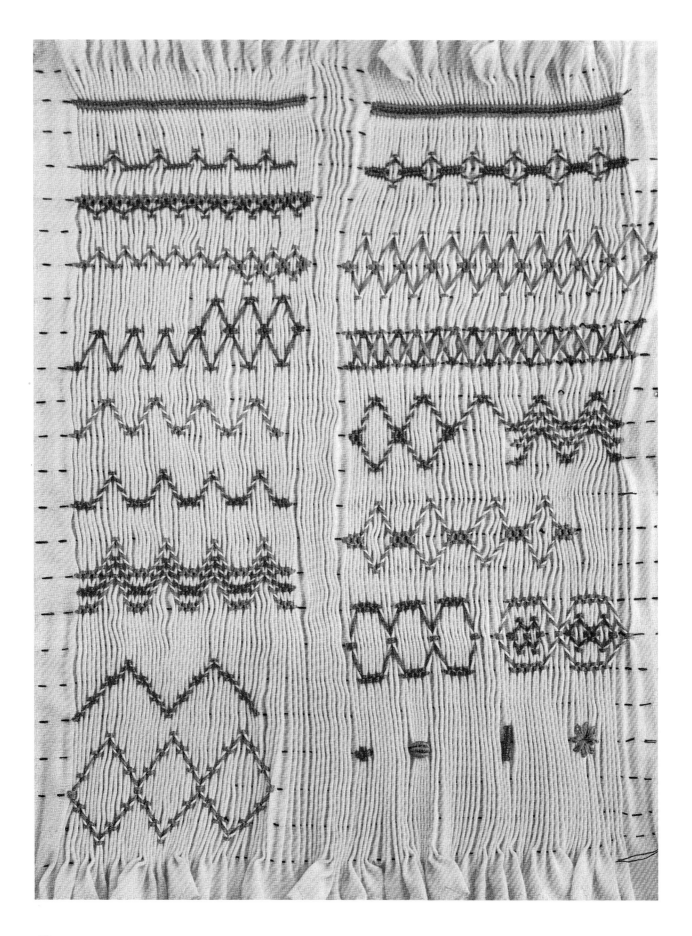

49

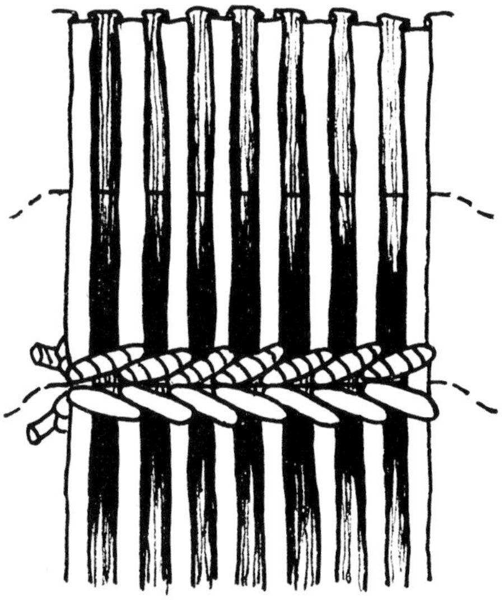

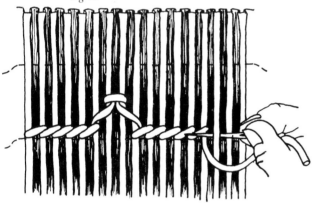

Fig 16

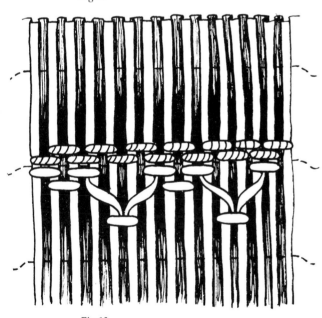

Fig 17

Combination stitches

Once the basic stitches have been mastered, they may be combined in an endless number of ways to produce a variety of combination stitches. This is what helps to make smocking such a creative and satisfying craft.

The following demonstrations of some combination stitches incorporated in the smocking designs of this book, represent only a few of the possibilities. Hopefully they will stimulate your own creativity by opening up a new world of design ideas, and enable you to reflect your individual style in your work.

Fig 16

Work one row of outline stitch a needle's width above the gathering thread row. Directly below this, work a row of stem stitch to give a mock chain or wheat effect, as shown on the photographed sampler on p. 49.

Variation

Work one row of outline stitch a needle's width above the gathering thread row. Directly below this, work a row of stem stitch and immediately below again, another row of outline stitch. This combination of stem and outline stitch, although very tight and without much stretch, is most effective when worked in two different colours (see p. 49).

Fig 17

Work a row of outline stitch, with a half space chevron between the outline stitches at regular intervals (see p. 49).

Variation

A variation of this stitch is a diamond-mock chain form. Work a row of outline stitch (a needle's width above the 2nd gathering thread row) with a half space chevron between the outline stitches at regular intervals. Directly below this, work a row of stem stitch with a half space chevron opposite the chevron of the row above, to form a diamond with a mock chain between the diamonds (see p. 49).

Fig 18

Starting with a bottom cable stitch, work a row of cable stitch. Directly below this, work a row that alternates between 3 cable stitches and a half space chevron, starting with a top cable stitch that will match the bottom cable stitch of the previous row. The finished effect is that of a cable flowerette between each chevron (see p. 49).

Variation

Work a row that alternates between 3 cable stitches and a half space chevron above and below the row of cable stitch. This will give a lace-like appearance, which is particularly effective if done in the centre of your design.

Fig 18

Fig 19

Starting with a bottom cable stitch (a needle's width above the 2nd gathering thread row), work a row that alternates between 3 cable stitches and a chevron (see p. 49). The chevron may be a full or a half space chevron.

Variations

Starting with a bottom cable stitch (a needle's width above the 2nd gathering thread row) work a row that alternates between 3 cable stitches and a chevron. The chevron may be a full or half space chevron. Directly below this, work another row that alternates between 3 cable stitches and a chevron, starting with a top cable stitch that will match the bottom cable stitch of the previous row. The finished effect will be that of a cable flowerette nestling between chevron diamonds (see p. 49).

This combination of stitches is very effective when worked in a large 'block', with one diamond repeated below the other. The combination also allows considerable stretch in the completed smocked piece. Another variation is to work alternate rows in different colours, one below the other.

This stitch combination is also most suitable for a crossover variation. Starting with a bottom cable stitch (a needle's width above the 2nd gathering thread row), work a row that alternates between 3 cable stitches and a chevron. The chevron may be a full space or a half space chevron. Over the top of this, starting with a top cable stitch a needle's width above the 1st gathering thread row, work another row that alternates between 3 cable stitches and a chevron.

Fig 20

Starting with a bottom cable stitch (a needle's width above the 2nd gathering thread row) work a row that alternates between 3 cable stitches at the top and bottom points of a chevron (see p. 49). The top point of the chevron may be a full or a half space above the gathering thread row on which you started. This combination of stitches will allow considerable stretch in the completed smocked piece.

Variations

This combination is also very suitable for a crossover variation. Starting with a bottom cable stitch (a needle's width above the 2nd gathering thread row), work a row that alternates between 3 cable stitches at the top and bottom points of a chevron. The top point of the chevron may be a full or a half space above the gathering thread row on which you started. Over the top of this and starting with a top cable stitch, work another row that alternates between 3 cable stitches at the top and bottom points of a chevron (see p. 49).

Starting with a bottom cable stitch, work a row that alternates between 3 cable stitches at the top and bottom points of a chevron. The top point of the chevron may be a full or a half space above the gathering thread row on which you started. Directly below this, work another row that alternates between 3 cable stitches at the top and bottom points of a chevron, starting with a top cable stitch that

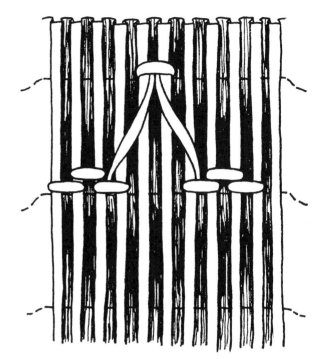

Fig 19

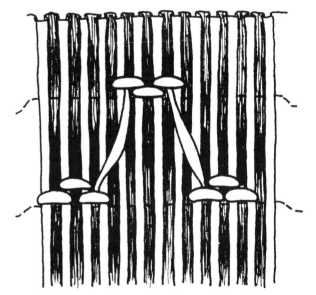

Fig 20

51

Alexandra in a smocked coat dress

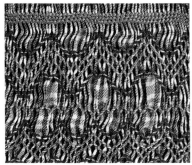

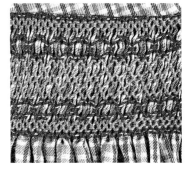

Lynne and Leigh-Anne in smocked shirts

Fig 21

will match the bottom cable stitch of the previous row (see p. 49). When worked in a large block, this combination gives the effect of a cable flowerette in the four corners of a diamond.

Another variation is to work alternate rows in different colours, one below the other.

Fig 21

Starting with a bottom cable stitch, work a row that alternates between 3 cable stitches at the top and bottom points of a full space 3-step wave (see p. 49).

Variations

Starting with a bottom cable stitch, work a row that alternates between 3 cable stitches at the top and bottom points of a full space 3-step wave. Directly below this, work another row that alternates between 3 cable stitches at the top and bottom points of a full space 3-step wave, starting with a top cable stitch that will match the bottom cable stitch of the previous row (see p. 49).

When worked in a large block, this combination gives the effect of a cable flowerette in the four corners of a 3-step diamond.

Another variation is to work alternate rows in different colours one below the other (see p. 49).

Fig 22

Fig 22

Starting with a bottom cable stitch (a needle's width above the 2nd gathering thread row), work 5 cable stitches. Next, work a full space 3-step wave to an 'up' point, a needle's width above the first gathering thread row. At this position, work a top cable stitch and then work a full space 3-step wave back to a needle's width above the gathering thread row on which you started. Work another 5 cable stitches. Continue to work across the row in this way (see p. 49).

Variations

Starting with a bottom cable stitch (a needle's width above the 2nd gathering thread row), work 5 cable stitches. Next, work a full space 3-step wave to an 'up' point. At this position work a top cable stitch and then work a full space 3-step wave back to a needle's width above the gathering thread row on which you started. Directly below this, work another row following the same sequence, but starting the row with a top cable that will match the bottom cable stitch of the previous row (see p. 49).

Another variation is to work alternate rows in different colours one below the other (see p. 49). The larger the number of rows worked one below the other, the tighter the smocked area becomes.

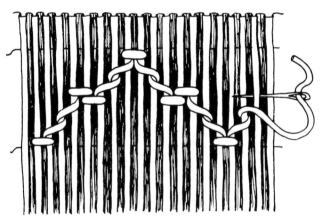

Fig 23

Fig 23

Work a bottom cable stitch a needle's width above the 3rd gathering thread row. Next, work a 2-step wave up to a point a needle's width above halfway between the 2nd and 3rd gathering thread rows. At this point work a top, then a bottom cable stitch. Continue by working another 2-step wave to a point a needle's width above the 2nd gathering thread row.

At this position, work a top cable stitch. Come down the trellis-cable stairstep using the same stitches and intervals as when you went up (see p. 49).

Fig 24

A variation of the stairstep stitch combination would be to work a 1-step wave instead of a 2-step wave between the cable stitches going up and down the stairstep (see p. 49).

A diamond variation of the stairstep stitch combination makes a very big and bold design that will need backsmocking or fill-in stitches to hold the pleats in the centre of the diamond together (see p. 49).

Fig 25a & b

Work a bottom cable stitch a needle's width above the gathering thread row. Next, work a full space 1-step wave to a point a needle's width above the 1st gathering thread row. At this point, work 7 cable stitches starting with a top cable stitch. Next, work a full space 1-step wave to a point a needle's width above the gathering thread row on which you started. Continue to work across the row in this way. Directly below this, work another row, following the same sequence of stitches and starting with a top cable stitch that will match the bottom cable of the previous row (see p. 49).

This large block design requires backsmocking or fill-in stitches to hold the pleats in the centre of the block together (see p. 49).

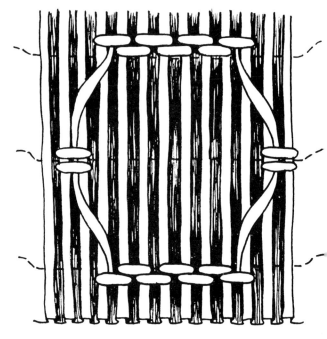

Fig 25a

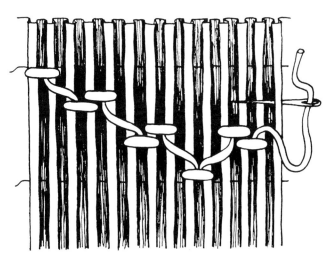

Fig 24

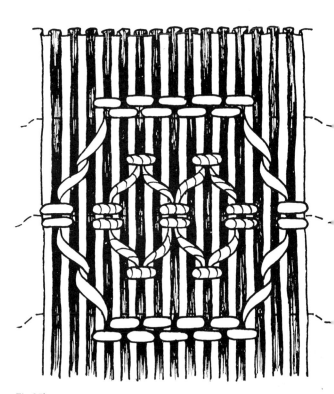

Fig 25b

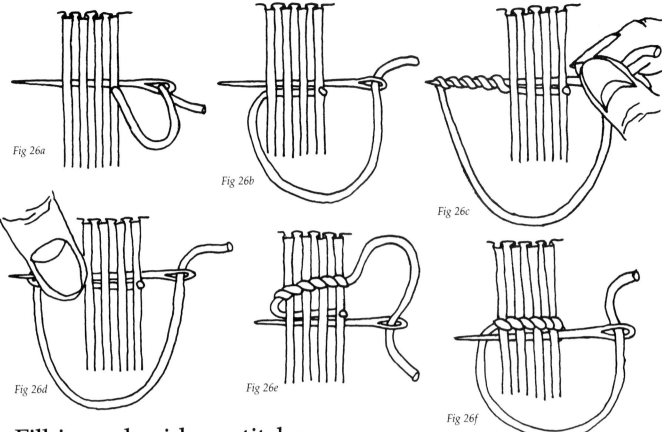

Fig 26a

Fig 26b

Fig 26c

Fig 26d

Fig 26e

Fig 26f

Fill-in embroidery stitches

Fill-in stitches may be used to give a design a focal point.

Rosebud

Rosebuds are most commonly used to fill in a diamond, and only 3 strands of embroidery thread are used.

Bring the needle up from the back of your work on the left-hand side of the first pleat. Run the needle through all the pleats in the centre of the diamond and pull through.

Re-insert the needle through all the pleats but before pulling through, wind the thread around the needle enough to fill the space the length of the diamond. Hold the 'wind' with the left hand, while pulling the thread through the pleats. Repeat this procedure three times to make a rosebud. Give the centre 'winding' an extra two or three winds. (Fig 26a, b, c, d, e, f)

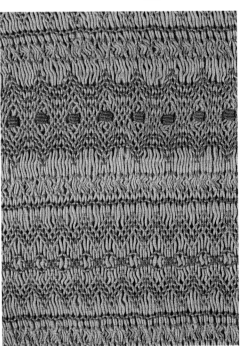

Opposite Alexandra in a conventional yoke dress with smocked cuffs and Nicole in a smocked dress with a frilled insert

Left *Detail of Alexandra's dress*

Above *Detail of Nicole's dress*

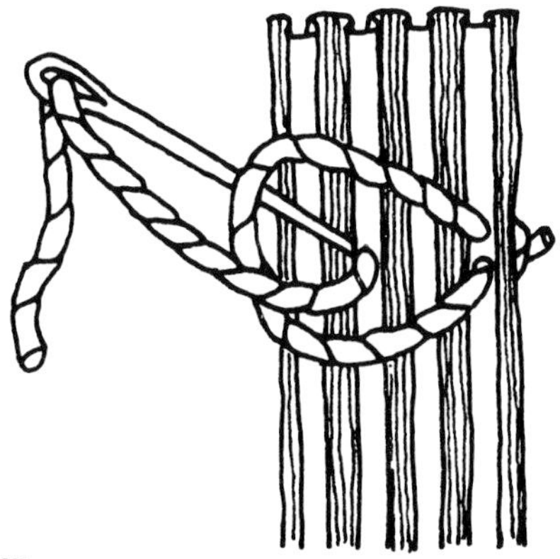

Fig 27a

Lazy daisy

This is an elongated chain stitch grouped to form a daisy. It is worked with 3 strands of embroidery thread. Begin at the centre of the lazy daisy. After each stitch is taken, return the needle to the pivotal point. *(Fig 27a & b)*

Double cable flowerette

Work 3 cable stitches, starting with a bottom cable stitch, thus using 4 pleats. Push the needle through all 4 pleats behind the 3 cable stitches and bring the needle out of the same hole as at starting point. Work 3 cable stitches starting with a top cable stitch that will match the bottom cable of the row above. Push the needle to the back of your work and end off the thread. *(Fig 28)*

Satin stitch

This is made by passing thread over and under the pleats in close parallel lines. *(Fig 28)*

Fig 27b

Fig 28

Construction principles

The following guidelines will assist you when constructing the various sections of your garment.

Seams

With the right sides of the fabric together, machine stitch the seam using the seam allowance specified in the pattern.

Seams are usually pressed open on the wrong side of the garment and the raw edges finished off with zig-zag stitching by machine.

French seams eliminate all raw edges. With the wrong sides of the fabric together, machine stitch the seam. On the inside of the garment, crease garment along the seam so that the right sides of the fabric are together. Stitch another seam. *(Fig 29)*

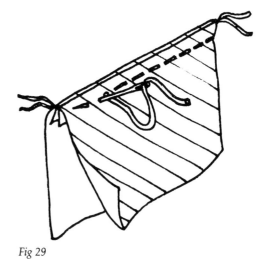

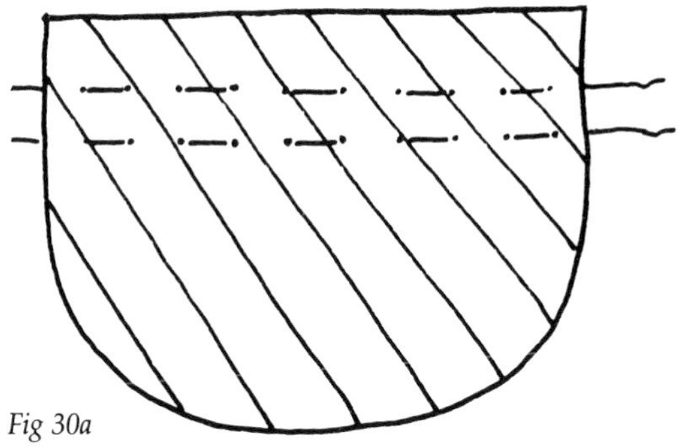

Fig 29

Pockets

Cut a piece of fabric three times the proposed finished width. (The depth of the pocket depends on individual taste and the size of the garment.) Make a rolled hem on the top edge. Draw up 3 to 4 gathering thread rows, approximately 2 cm (¾ inch) from the rolled hem edge, and smock a design of your choice.

Turn under the edges of the pocket 1 cm (½ inch), curving the bottom corners if desired. Stitch the pocket into place. *(Fig 30a & b)*

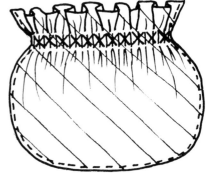

Fig 30a

Bias strip neck edge

A bias strip is cut at a 45° angle to the selvage of the fabric. It is used to finish off curves.

A neck edge bias strip should be approximately 32 cm (12½ inches) long and 3 cm (1¼ inches) wide. With right sides together, pin and baste the strip to the neck edge. The strip should extend approximately 0,5 cm (¼ inch) beyond the garment edge at the centre back.

Stitch the bias strip to the garment. Trim and clip the seam. Turn the strip to the inside and slipstitch into place. At the centre back, turn the raw edge of the bias strip under, fold ends to the inside of the garment and slipstitch into place. Finish with a hook and eye.

Fig 30b

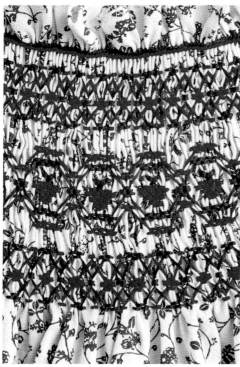

Right *Nicole in a conventional yoke dress smocked to the waist*

Opposite *Leigh-Anne in a smocked sundress with bound armholes*

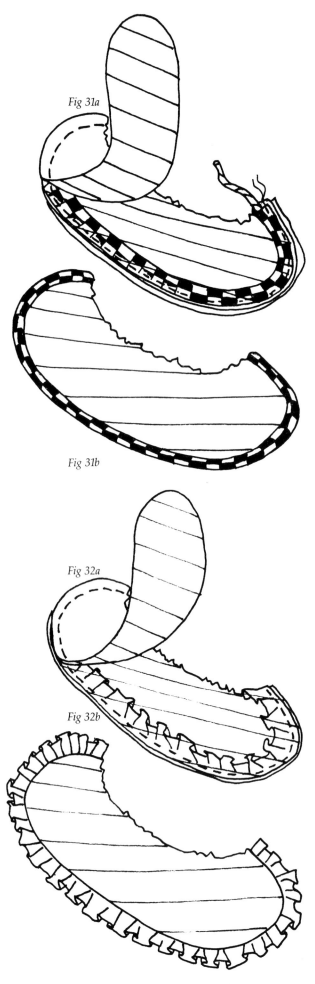

Fig 31a

Fig 31b

Fig 32a

Fig 32b

Collars

A collar gives a finished look to a garment and must fit a neckline to perfection. Collars should meet at the centre front and back. Machine stitch the collars with right sides together. Trim and grade seams to prevent a ridge when pressing. Clip the edges, turn the collars right side out and press them, keeping the corners even. Following the instructions accompanying your pattern, baste and then machine stitch the collar to the garment along the neck edge. Interfacing may be used.

Collar with a bias facing

Cut a 4 cm (1½ inch) wide bias strip the length of the collar plus 2,5 cm (1 inch). Baste the bias strip to the neck edge over the collar, easing the bias strip. All the raw edges should be together. Turn in the ends of the bias strip 2,5 cm (1 inch) at the centre back and slipstitch into place. Sew along the basting stitches. Trim and clip the edge. Turn in the free edge of the bias strip and slipstitch to the inside, so that it lies flat.

There are several ways of finishing off a collar edge:

- *Corded piping*   - *Lace trim*   - *Embroidery stitches*   - *Frill*

Collar with corded piping

Cut two bias strips about 25 cm - 30 cm (10 - 12 inches) long. Place the cording in the centre of the wrong side of the bias strip. Fold the bias strip over the cording and stitch very close to the cording on the right side of the fabric with a zipper foot.

Trim the seam and clip it at short intervals. Pin the corded piping to the right side of the collar with the raw edges together. Stitch the piping to the collar using a 1 cm (½ inch) seam, then pin the collar lining to the collar with right sides together. The corded piping will be between the two collar pieces.

Stitch from the wrong side of the collar on top of the first stitching. Trim and clip the edge. Turn the collar right side out and press well. (Fig 31a & b)

Collar with lace trim

Cut the lace about twice the length of the collar's outside edge. Run two rows of machine gathering stitches along the length of the lace, 1 cm (½ inch) from the raw edge. Pull up the lace so that it measures the same as the outside edge of the collar.

Pin the lace to the right side of the collar with raw edges together and stitch into place using a 1 cm (½ inch) seam. Pin the collar lining to the collar with right sides together. The lace will be between the two collar pieces and turned to the inside. Stitch from the wrong side of the collar on top of the first stitching. Trim and clip the seam, turn the collar right side out and press well. (Fig 32a & b)

Collar with embroidery stitches

Decorative embroidery stitches may be used to enhance the collar.

Construct the collar as previously described and press well. Measure 3 times round the completed collar, add 3 cm (1¼ inches) and cut a piece of embroidery thread of this length. Strip the embroidery thread and separate 3 strands. Make a knot at one end and select one of the following stitches:

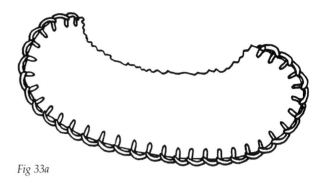

Fig 33a

Simple blanket stitch

Come up from the wrong to the right side of the collar and work from left to right around it, holding the thread under the left thumb while making the stitch. Insert the needle a little to the right for each successive stitch.

To keep the embroidery stitches a consistent size, use the ridge edge (the result of trimming the seam on the wrong side) and the outer edge of the collar as a guide. Embroidery stitches are only done on the right side of the collar. *(Fig 33a)*

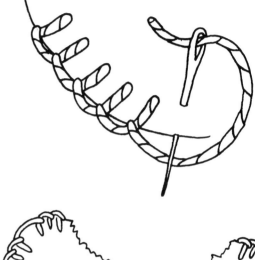

Long-short-long blanket stitch

Using the same method as for simple blanket stitch, vary the length of the stitch in groupings of a long stitch, a short stitch and a long stitch at regular intervals along the edge of the collar. *(Fig 33b)*

Short-long-short blanket stitch

Using the same method as for simple blanket stitch, vary the length of the stitch in groupings of a short stitch, a long stitch and a short stitch at regular intervals along the edge of the collar. *(Fig 33c)*

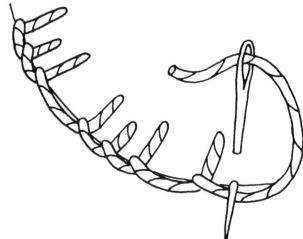

Fig 33b

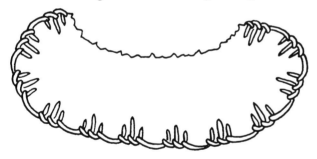

Fig 33c

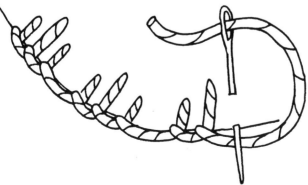

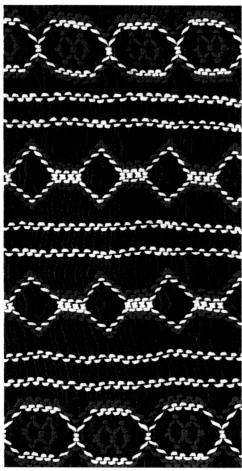

Opposite *Alexandra in a conventional yoke dress smocked to the waist*

Left *Sandra in a circular necked blouse*

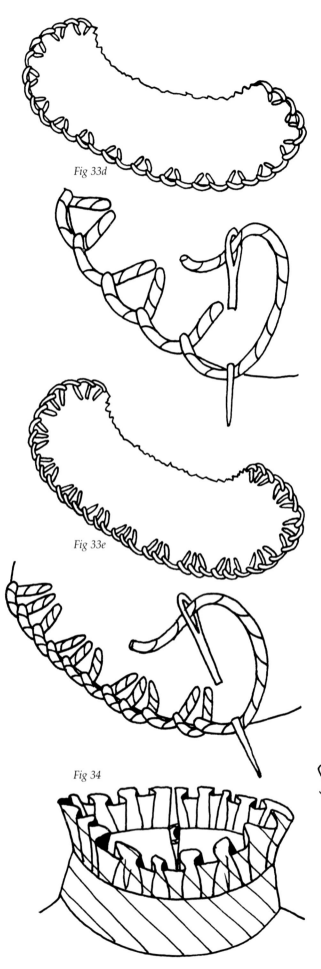

Fig 33d

Fig 33e

Fig 34

Slanting blanket stitch

Using the same method as for simple blanket stitch, vary the stitches by slanting the needle to form a 'v'. Insert and point the needle to the right and then insert and point the needle to the left. *(Fig 33d)*

Variation

As a variation of the slanting blanket stitch, add a straight stitch in the middle. *(Fig 33e)*

Outline stitch

Come up from the wrong side of the collar, about 0,5 cm (¼ inch) from the finished edge of the collar. As for outline stitch, make small even stitches that touch each other. The thread always falls to the right of the needle. *(Fig 33f)*

Collar with a frill

Finish off the edges of the frill with a rolled hem. Gather the frill along its length. With the right sides together, pin and then baste the frill to the collar. Stitch the collar facing to the collar, leaving the neck edge free.

Trim and clip the seam edges, turn to the right side and press. Pin the collar to the neck edge with right sides together and stitch into place. Clip the curves and press the seam towards the collar.

Turn under the free edge of the collar and slipstitch into place. Press well. *(Fig 34)*

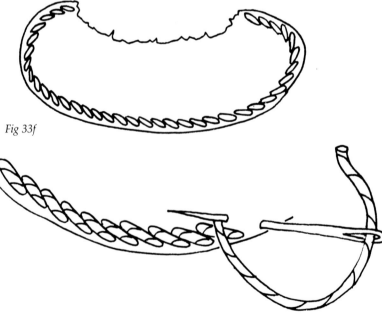

Fig 33f

Placket

A placket is a strip of fabric used to bind the raw edges of a slit which has been cut in a garment to facilitate putting it on and taking it off.

If a centre back placket is planned, 3 pleats on either side of the centre back marking (i.e. 6 pleats at the centre back) should be left unsmocked. Make a slit down the centre back pleat. *(Fig 35a & b)*

Cut a strip of fabric approximately 5 cm (2 inches) wide and twice the length of the opening. Sew the strip to the garment with right sides together, pulling the slashed opening into a straight line as you do so. *(Fig 35c)*

Fold the free edge of the strip under 0,5 cm (¼ inch). Fold the strip in half and slipstitch to the garment. *(Fig 35d)*

Turn the left side of the placket to the inside and baste across the top. The right side is not turned to the inside. *(Fig 35e)*

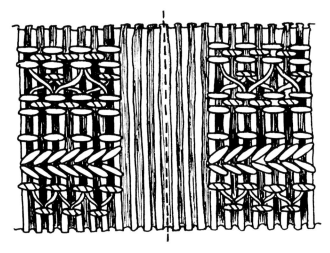

Fig 35a

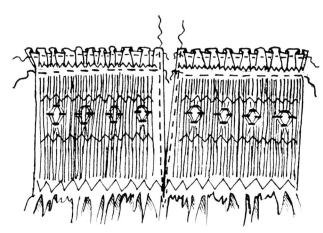

Fig 35b

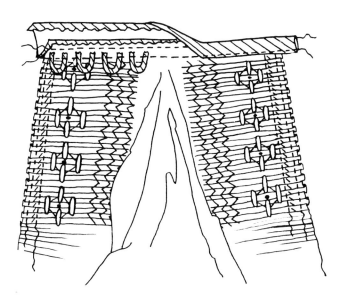

Fig 35d

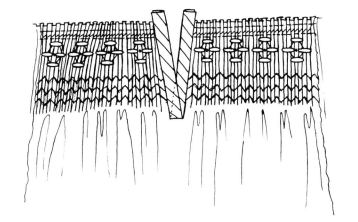

Fig 35e

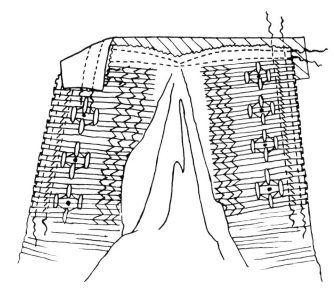

Fig 35c

Nerine in an adult's blouse smocked from the shoulders

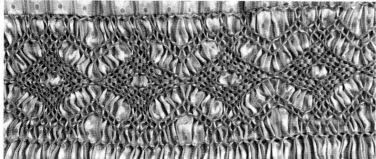

Ayesha in a waisted smocked dress

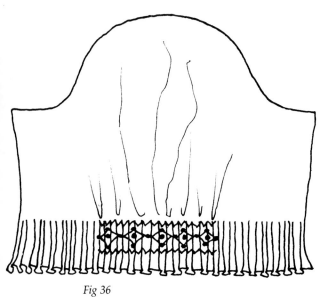

Fig 36

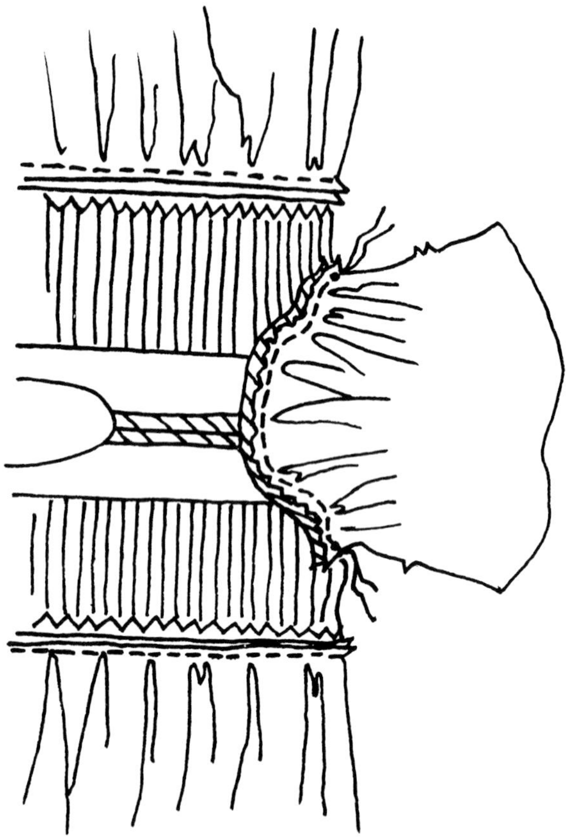

Sleeves

Sleeves on smocked dresses are completed by one of the following methods:

- *Smocked sleeve*
- *Shirring elastic*
- *Bias band*
- *Lace edging*

Smocked sleeve

Before putting a sleeve through the smocking pleater, make a rolled hem at the sleeve edge or attach lace to it. The width of a sleeve suitable for smocking should be 3 times the wrist or upper arm measurement.

Thread the smocking pleater with 3 or 4 gathering threads for a child's puffed sleeve, and 5 to 7 for an adult's sleeve. Roll the sleeve onto a dowel stick and feed it through the pleater. Keep a little of the frill on the outside left-hand side of the machine.

Cut the threads and knot them to prevent the pleats from pulling out. Leave 8 pleats on either side of the sleeve seam and smock your chosen design. Remove the gathering threads. *(Fig 36)*

On the edge to be attached to the garment, make a row of gathering stitches along the seam line, between the notches. Add another row of gathering stitches 0,5 cm (¼ inch) above this. Pin the sleeve to the armhole of the garment, matching the notches, and pull up the gathering stitches to ease in the fullness. Stitch along the seam line. Pull out the gathering stitches. Overlock the sleeve edge and press the seam towards the sleeve. *(Fig 37)*

Shirring elastic

Make a rolled hem and finish off the lower edge of the sleeve by sewing 3 rows of shirring elastic by machine, approximately 2 cm (¾ inch) from the finished edge.

Fig 37

Bias band

The bottom edge of a puffed sleeve may be finished off with a bias band. Cut a bias band about 3 cm (1¼ inches) wide and about 4 cm (1½ inches) longer than the arm measurement. With right sides together, stitch the narrow edges of the band to form a circle. Make a row of gathering stitches along the lower sleeve edge. Pin the right side of the sleeve edge to the right side of the band.

Pull up the sleeve gathers to fit the band and stitch the bias band and sleeve together on the sleeve side. Gathers must be evenly distributed around the band. Turn under the free raw edge of the bias band and slipstitch into place on the wrong side of the sleeve. *(Fig 38a, b, c)*

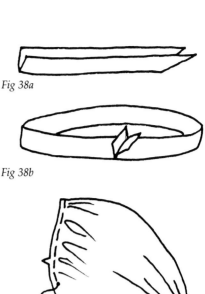

Fig 38a

Fig 38b

Lace edging

Sew on lace before smocking or completing the edge with shirring elastic, as previously described.

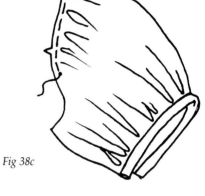

Fig 38c

Cuffs

Cut a strip of fabric 7 cm (2¾ inches) wide and the length of the slash line on the sleeve, plus 3 cm (1¼ inches). Turn under 1 cm (½ inch) on three sides of the facing and stitch. Baste the centre of the facing over the slash line.

Stitch 1 cm (½ inch) from the basting at the seam line to a point at the top and back down the other side, in the same manner. Slash to the point of stitching. Turn facing to the inside and press. Hem the facing to the sleeve and gather the sleeve. Stitch and attach the cuff to the lower edge of the sleeve. *(Fig 39)*

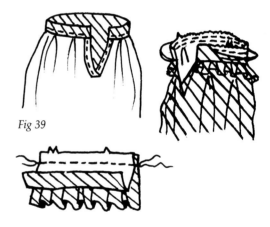

Fig 39

Butterfly frill

Attach lace to the straight edge of the butterfly frill. Gather the curved edges of the frill 0,5 cm (¼ inch) inside the seam line. With the right sides together, pin the gathered sleeve frill to the armhole edge. Baste into place and then machine stitch. *(Fig 40)*

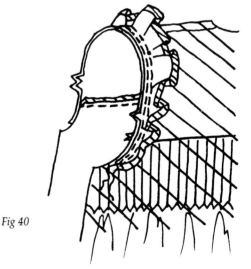

Fig 40

Incorporation of smocking

There are several ways of incorporating smocking into the garment.

Conventional yoke dress

1. Smock the skirt front and back using a design of your choice.

2. Remove the gathering threads from the smocked piece, except at the level of the first row of smocking.

3. Place correct pattern piece on the blocked smocking. *(Fig 41)*

4. Cut out the armholes. Five pleats should have been left free of smocking on either side of the smocked piece, so that it is not necessary to cut into the smocking when cutting out the armholes.

5. Fold piece in half and insert a pin to mark the centre front.

6. Fold yoke piece in half and insert a pin to mark centre front.

7. Place right sides of smocked piece and yoke together, matching pins at centre front markings. Pin armhole edges of yoke to armhole edges of smocked piece and stretch smocking to fit yoke perfectly on either side of centre front markings. *(Fig 42)*

8. Baste yoke to smocked front, then attach yoke by sewing just above gathering thread row, at level of the first row of smocking. *(Fig 43)* Trim seam and finish off by machine with zigzag stitching.

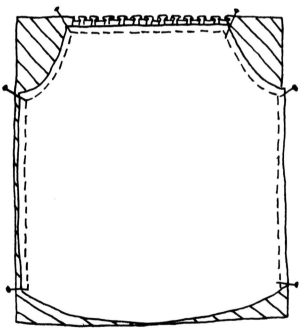

Fig 41

Opposite *Lynne and Leigh-Anne in conventional yoke dresses*

73

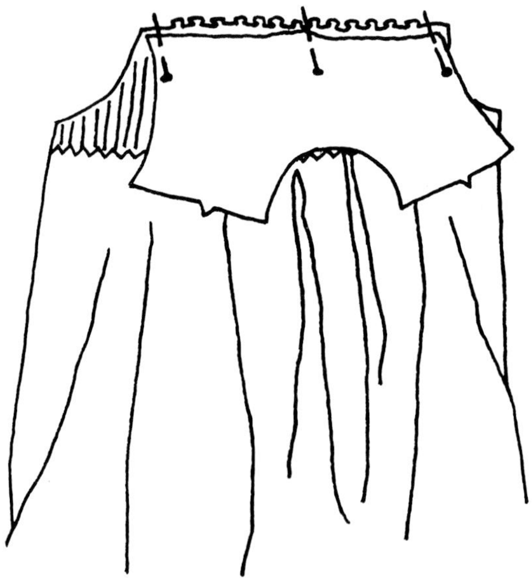

Back yokes

Make a placket (as described on p. 67) at the centre back of the skirt. Pin the back yoke to the skirt with right sides together. Attach the yoke to the smocked piece by sewing just above the gathering thread row, at the level of the first row of smocking. Trim the seam and finish it off by machine with zigzag stitching. *(Fig 44a & b)*

Shoulder seams

With the right sides together, sew the shoulder seams of the yokes. Press the seams open and finish them off by machine with zigzag stitching.

Pin the sleeve to the armhole of the dress with right sides together. Match underarm seam to side seam and the centre of the sleeve to the shoulder seam of the dress. Stitch along the seam line. Finish the seams off by machine with zigzag stitching.

Construct the collar or frill and attach it to the dress with a bias neck band. Put up the hem of the garment using a blindstitch or slipstitch. Press the garment. At the centre back, make buttonholes on the yoke and sew on the buttons. If necessary, sew press-studs onto the placket.

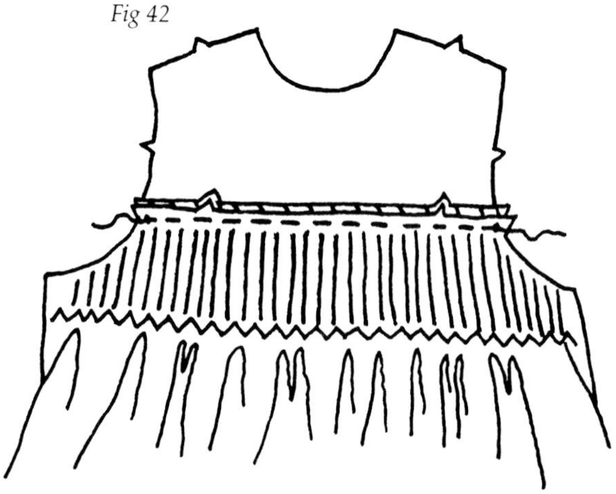

Fig 42

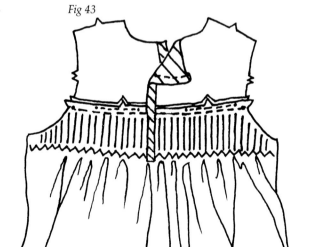

Fig 43

Fig 44a

Fig 44b

Smocked insert

The insert may be any shape or size and any commercial pattern with an insert portion is suitable. *(Fig 45)* The amount of fabric you need to smock for the insert is easier to calculate if the insert portion of the commercial pattern has no pleats, tucks or gathers.

A smocked insert that is to be used as a decorative trim may be of a different fabric to the remainder of the garment. In this case, you may have to adjust the ratio for the amount of fabric allowed for each centimetre or inch of completed smocking.

As a general rule, 8 cm (3¼ inches) of fabric gives 2,5 cm (1 inch) of completed smocking. The ratio of the length of fabric to the length of completed smocking varies from 6 : 1 for fine fabric to 2,5 : 1 for heavier fabrics.

Always place the commercial pattern piece across the complete insert, to ensure that the insert has enough fullness to cover the pattern piece without stretching the pleats too much. Two pieces may be joined together to make up the required length or width of fabric for pleating.

Fig 45

Preparation of fabric

Press fabric to remove all creases and wrinkles. Check that the crosswise and lengthwise threads are at right angles to each other. Cut off selvages. Look at insert piece and decide which way you wish the pleats to lie, i.e. vertically or horizontally in the inserted area. Measure the widest part of the insert pattern piece, triple the measurement if it is a 'whole' piece and multiply the measurement by 6 if it is a 'half' piece, i.e. a piece that would normally be placed on the fold.

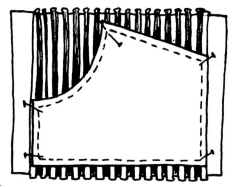

Fig 46

Cut out a square or rectangular shape according to these measurements and gather up the required number of rows, using either the smocking pleater or dots. Tie off the gathering threads at each end of your prepared fabric, straighten the pleats and pull them out to measure approximately 3 cm to 5 cm (1¼ to 2 inches) shorter than the desired width on completion.

To minimize smocking in areas that will be cut away in the final construction of your garment, use the commercial pattern piece to mark out roughly any area on the prepared fabric that will be cut away after smocking is complete, such as neck curves, armhole curves or curves resulting from the shape of the prepared insert. However, do not cut these areas until the smocking has been completed. *(Fig 46)*

On completion, remove the gathering threads. To block the piece to the desired width, place the commercial pattern insert piece over the smocking and stretch to fit the pattern. Mark the smocked insert where it is to be cut.

Do two rows of machine stitching – one on the marking and one just inside the first row – to prevent the smocking from unravelling. Your insert piece is now ready to be cut out. *(Fig 47a, b, c)*

Continue to make up the garment according to the instructions in the commercial pattern. Reinforce the seam that joins the smocked insert to the remainder of the garment with a double seam and zigzag stitching.

Attaching an insert without curves

After the smocked insert has been blocked, run a basting thread along the top and bottom rows of the smocking, as a stitching guide. Baste the right sides of the garment and insert together. Stitch along the basting stitch guide.

There are three methods of attaching an insert that has no curves to be cut away:

- *Piping (boy's shirt)*
- *Directly onto other garment pieces*
- *Contrasting bands*

Attaching a frilled insert

When constructing a garment with a frill on the sides of an insert (i.e. where the frill is joined to the remainder of the garment), press the seam towards the centre of the inserted panel. This will ensure that the frill lies flat. However, because the panel is smocked, the seam will lie away from the panel and the frill will flop forwards onto the panel. To solve this problem, turn the seam towards the panel and slipstitch on the inside to hold it in position. This will ensure that the frill lies flat.

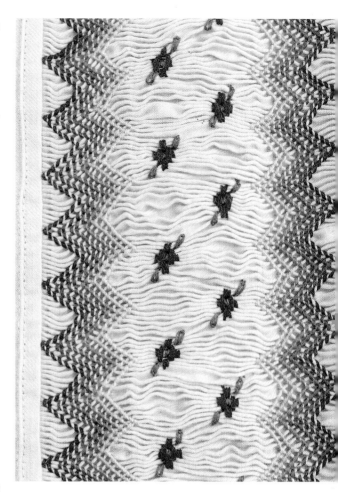

Opposite *Leigh-Anne in a dress with a vertically smocked insert*

Above *Detail of insert*

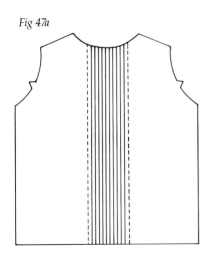

Fig 47a

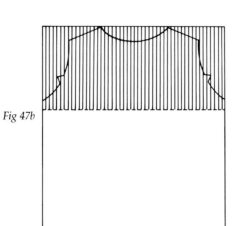

Fig 47b

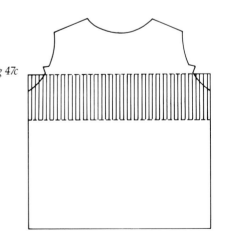

Fig 47c

Circular neck garment

The neck edge of a circular neck garment may be bound, ruffled or scooped out to varying degrees. It may have a front or back opening with or without a placket or no opening at all, as in the case of a scooped neck garment.

The smocking of a circular neck garment will require a great deal of fullness on a light-weight fabric – plan on using 12-16 rows on the yoke and half this number on the cuffs. For a medium weight fabric, plan on 6-8 rows of smocking on the yoke and cuffs.

Any fabric that has a check, a stripe or a stripe with a superimposed pattern is unsuitable for smocking a circular neck garment, as it is practically impossible to keep the stripes or checks running out radially from the neck edge.

When working out a design to smock on a circular neck garment, you should design in terms of groups of rows. The first group is closest to the neck edge, so choose a set of stitches that do not expand very much, so as to give maximum control to the fullness. The middle group should be the decorative set, as this area should be the focal point of the design. The last group should have deep wave or diamond stitches, as this set must have the most stretch. An adult's circular neck design should have this set of stitches at least two rows of gathering threads deep, so that the smocked yoke of the garment will spread evenly over the shoulders.

As a general rule, it is most impractical to plan a geometric smocking design in which the stitches have to meet at regular intervals, one row below the other, over a depth of more than three gathering thread rows. This is because the yoke widens as it approaches the armholes and therefore the number of pleats increases as well. In other words, change your design approximately every three gathering thread rows.

Before working all the way round the yoke with any particular row, first work 7,5 cm (3 inches) or so of your complete design. This will show most accurately what your design will look like once completed. At this stage it is not a major task to change your stitch combination or adjust your colours.

Circular neck construction

The following basic instructions should be used when constructing a circular neck smock. The same instructions apply to construction of circular neck garments for all age groups.

1. In all cases, use a commercial pattern for a smocked circular neck garment.

2. Begin your project by pressing the fabric to remove all creases and wrinkles. Check that the crosswise and lengthwise threads are at right angles to one another and cut off the selvages.

3. Cut out your garment according to the instructions accompanying your pattern and mark the centre back, centre front and the centre of each sleeve. If you wish to have a centre front or

centre back placket, the centre front or centre back of the pattern piece should be on the fold of the fabric when you cut out your garment. Although the neckline is curved, the fabric is cut out on the straight. To get the neckline to curve, the smocking has to be worked so that the yoke will fan into a curved shape.

4.   The following table provides a useful guide for determining the circumference to which the raw neck edge should be drawn to form the 'doughnut' shape before smocking.

Garment size	Circumference of neck at raw neck edge
Infant	24,0 cm (9½ inches)
Size 1 - 2	25,5 cm (10 inches)
Size 3 - 4	27,0 cm (10½ inches)
Size 5 - 8	28,0 - 29,0 cm (11-11½ inches)

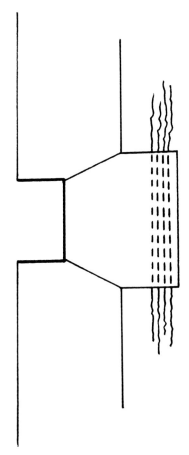

Fig 48

Preparation of fabric for smocking

Instructions for drawing up the fabric into the pleated 'canvas' on which the smocking design is worked, have been given on p. 15-18. However, certain aspects applicable to circular neck garments in particular will be dealt with here.

Sleeves

1.   Should you wish to smock on the cuffs of a garment, particularly one with short sleeves, it is most important to remember that the sleeves must be put through the smocking pleater before the yoke.

2.   Make a rolled hem on the cuff edge before transferring dots or gathering up the pleats.

3.   Ensure that the gathering threads on the cuffs are longer than you would normally have them. This will allow sufficient thread at both ends of the sleeve piece (after gathering up the threads on the sleeve) to enable the sleeve to be stretched out flat, so stretching the gathers before the yoke is put through the pleater. *(Fig 48)*

4.   After the yoke has been put through the pleater, the gathering threads on the sleeves may be drawn up again to form the pleats.

5.   Use a variation of the smocking design used (or planned) for the yoke and begin smocking on the 8th pleat from the seam edge. The last row of smocking should be approximately 2,5 cm (1 inch) from the edge of the cuff.

6.   When completing the construction of this part of your garment, sew down the length of the sleeve, straight past the smocking to the rolled hem, taking care not to catch the smocking in the seam.

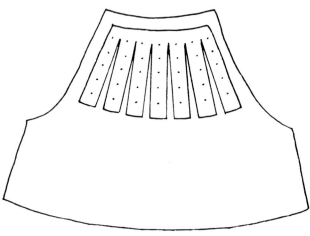

Fig 49

7. The following are alternatives to a smocked cuff:

A frill made by sewing around the cuff approximately 2,5 cm (1 inch) from its rolled hem with shirring elastic in the bobbin rather than thread.

An elastic threaded through the hem of the sleeve.

An elastic threaded through a casing approximately 2,5 cm (1 inch) from the rolled hem at the edge of the cuff.

A conventional cuff into which the sleeve is gathered or pleated.

For more detailed descriptions of these constructions, see p. 71.

Yoke

Transferring the smocking dots

1. Having marked the centre front, centre back and the centre of each sleeve, transfer the required number of rows of dots, making sure that at the centre markings, the rows of dots that can be lined up vertically are at right angles to the neck edge (i.e. parallel to the grain of your fabric).

2. In order to achieve this transferral of dots in a curve, you may have to slash the dot pattern transfer sheet before transferring the dots to your fabric. This will be particularly necessary in a longer smocking design. *(Fig 49)*

3. If you plan to use a geometric smocking design with the smocking stitches meeting at regular intervals one row below the other, there must obviously be the same number of pleats from the neck edge to the bottom of the yoke. In a longer design in particular, there may be some unpleated space on each side of the sleeve seams towards the under-arm area. This space will eventually be on the inside of the garment and will be lost in the folds once the smocking is complete and the gathering threads have been removed.

4. Once the dots have been transferred to the fabric, sew front to front sleeve and back to back sleeve by machine, taking care to match all the rows of dots.

5. Gather up the threads and tie the ends as described on p. 15-18, so that the pleats at the neck edge form a 'doughnut' shape and then radiate out towards the bottom of the yoke.

6. Set the pleats with steam. Following your previously worked out design, smock the yoke of your circular neck garment.

Smocking pleater

Instructions for drawing up pleats for a circular neck garment vary slightly according to whether there is to be a centre back/centre front placket or a centre back/centre front seam. Cut out the garment and mark the centre front/centre back and centre sleeve.

With a placket (no centre back or centre front seam)

1. Machine stitch the front to the sleeve fronts and back to one sleeve back, i.e. one sleeve to sleeve back seam is left open.

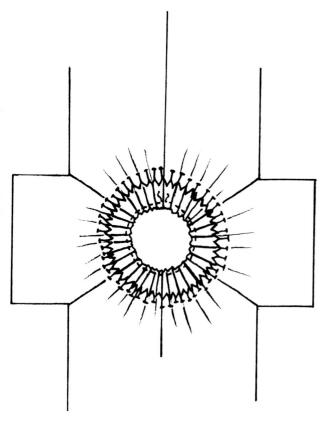

Fig 50

2. Finish off these seams and press them towards the centre sleeve.

3. Roll your fabric onto the dowel stick starting at the back/sleeve back opening and making sure that when your fabric reaches the centre front, centre back and centre sleeve markings, the dowel stick is at right angles to the neck edge (i.e. parallel to the grain of your fabric).

4. There should be no folds in the yoke rolled onto the dowel stick at the neck edge, although there may well be quite large folds in the fabric at the lower edge of the yoke, especially towards the under-arm areas.

5. The yoke should be rolled onto the dowel stick so as to ensure that only the yoke area goes through the pleater, i.e. the left-hand side of the pleater is used and the bulk of the garment fabric is outside the pleater.

6. When putting the yoke through the pleater, make sure there is a gathering thread close to the raw edge of the neck. This gathering thread will not be used for smocking, but will make it easier to smock on the second gathering thread, as it lies flat with no ruffles immediately above it.

7. Pull up the gathering threads into a 'doughnut' shape at the neck edge and adjust the pleats so that they are looser at the bottom of the yoke and tighter at the neck edge.

8. Machine stitch the back/sleeve back seam, taking care to match the gathering threads. Finish off the seam.

9. Mark the centre back or centre front, depending on where the placket is to go on the finished garment.

10. Leave three pleats on either side of this marking and start smocking your design between these two markings, working all the way round the yoke.

With a centre back or centre front seam

The pleating of a circular yoke with a centre back/centre front seam differs from the pleating of a circular yoke with a placket as follows:

1. Machine stitch front to sleeve fronts and back to sleeve backs.

2. Leave the centre front or centre back open over the entire length of the garment. Finish off the seams and press them towards the centre sleeves.

3. Roll the fabric onto a dowel stick, starting at the centre back or centre front (whichever is applicable), making sure that when the fabric reaches the centre back, centre front and centre sleeve markings, the dowel stick is at right angles to the neck edge, (i.e. parallel to the grain of your fabric).

4. Once the pleats are drawn up into the desired 'doughnut' shape, leave 5 pleats at the centre front/centre back seam edges and begin smocking your design between these two markings, working all the way round the yoke.

82

Finishing construction of the garment

You are now ready to finish your garment construction, beginning with the important process of blocking.

Blocking

Once your smocking is complete, pull out the gathering threads, except those at the neck edge and at the level of the first row of smocking. Block the yoke into a full circle. It is easier and advisable to block your garment at this stage – before the side seams are stitched.

Blocking is done by carefully spreading the smocked yoke out evenly into a full circle and pinning it to an ironing board. It is a useful technique to stick pins into the ironing board through the smocking, at a vertical angle at the lowest point of each of the zigzags in the last row of smocking. This prevents the lowest points of these zigzags acquiring a 'rounded' look, which is particularly inclined to happen in a yoke with many rows of smocking.

Steam the fabric, without touching the smocking with the iron. Alternatively, the smocking may be left attached to the ironing board, sprayed with water and allowed to dry overnight. *(Fig 50)*

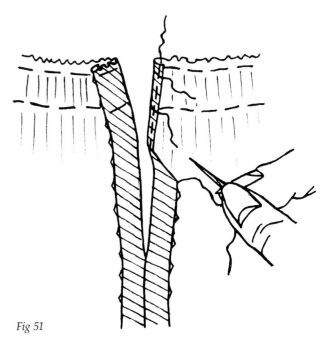

Fig 51

Neck openings

(For construction of a placket, see p. 67.)

Centre front or centre back opening

When you smock the yoke, leave 5 pleats on either side of the centre back seam unsmocked. For convenience, we will deal here with a centre back opening.

Sew up the centre back seam to just below the lowest stitch of smocking in the last row. Press the seam open. Fold over the centre back edge an amount equal to the width of the seam up to the neck edge. Baste into place. *(Fig 51)*

Sew buttons on the right-hand side and make thread loops at the edge of the opening on the left-hand side, to correspond with the buttons. *(Fig 52)*

Sew up the rest of your garment using the instructions accompanying your pattern. Leave the finishing of the neck edge until last.

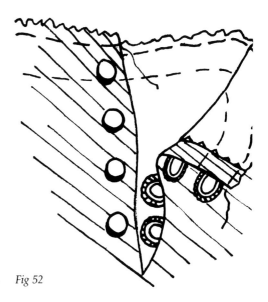

Fig 52

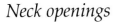

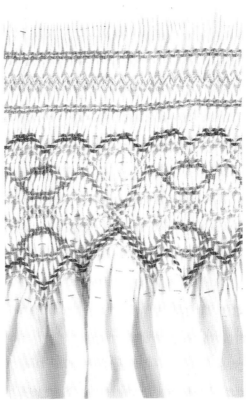

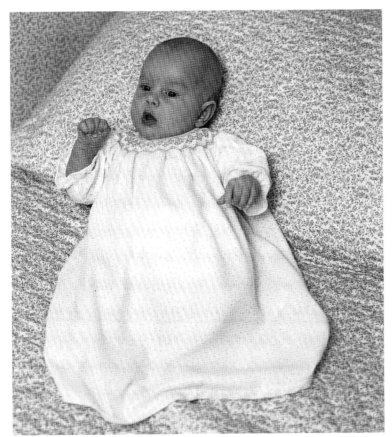

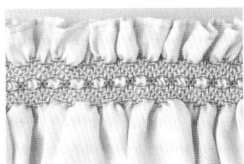

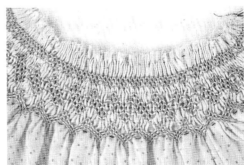

Opposite *Megan in a circular necked coat dress with smocked pockets*

Above left *Michaela in a smocked bonnet*

Below *Ina in a smocked circular necked nightdress*

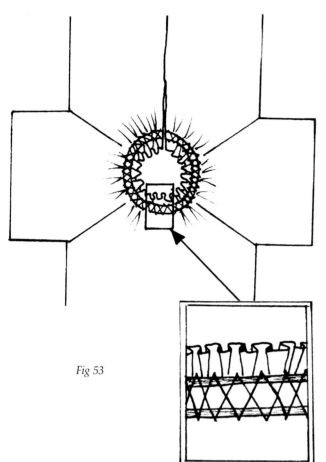

Fig 53

Neck edge

The neck edge may be scooped out to any degree and may be finished off in three ways:

Ruffle

For a ruffled neck, the neck edge should be made into a rolled hem after the front, sleeves and back have been sewn together, and before the gathering threads of the yoke have been drawn up. It is advisable to leave the centre front or centre back seam open, so as not to have an unsightly join at the edge of the ruffle. The first row of smocking should start approximately 7,5 cm (3 inches) from the rolled hem edge.

After you have completed your smocking you may find it useful to work several rows of cable stitch on the wrong side of the garment, at the level of the first row of smocking on the right side. This back-smocking will balance the tension on both sides of the fabric, so that the ruffle will stand up straight rather than roll forward. It will also give added strength to the neck edge.

If, despite this precaution the ruffle still rolls forward, it may be necessary to run a row of shirring elastic at the level of the first row of smocking. If even more control is needed, add a piece of elastic to the inside top row of smocking, holding it in place with herringbone stitch done over the elastic, so that the elastic moves freely in a herringbone 'casing'. (Fig 53)

Binding

Use the gathering threads which were left in at the neck edge and at the level of the first row of smocking at the blocking stage to adjust your final neck measurement.

Cut a bias strip 5 cm (2 inches) wide and the length 1 cm to 2 cm (½ to ¾ inch) longer than the final neck measurement. Fold the binding in half lengthwise with the wrong sides together and press. Attach the binding to the neck edge on the right side, with both free edges of the binding at the neck edge. Leave an overlap of binding of approximately 0,5 cm to 1 cm (approximately ¼ inch) at the neck opening. (Fig 54)

Use the gathering thread at the level of the first row of smocking as a guide and sew just above it when attaching the binding. This will enable you to attach the binding neatly above the first row of smocking. Trim the seam evenly, then roll the binding tightly over the edge and slipstitch on the inside. At the neck opening, turn over the overlap of binding and slipstitch it into place.

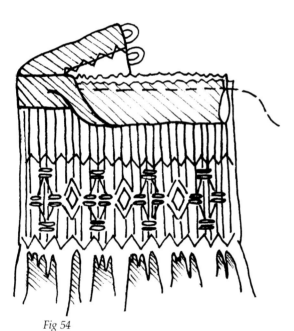

Fig 54

Bound neck with tie ends

This is a variation of a bound neck. The bias strip is cut much longer than the final neck measurement to allow sufficient fabric to tie the ends into a bow.

Cut the bias strip 2,5 cm (1 inch) wide. Do not fold the strip in half lengthwise before attaching to the neck edge. Sew binding to neck edge with right sides together. Trim the neck edge. *(Fig 55a)* Fold the binding in half lengthwise with right sides together. Stitch a seam from the neck opening edge to the end of the bias strip. *(Fig 55b)*

With a needle, fasten a strong thread to the raw end of the bias strip. Draw forward through the fold, turning the binding ends right side out.

Turn under the remainder of the binding round the neck, roll tightly over the edge and then slipstitch into place on the wrong side. Turn in 0,5 cm (¼ inch) at the end of the ties and slipstitch closed. *(Fig 55c)*

This method of completing a neck edge is particularly applicable to finishing off a baby's nightgown, or an adult's scooped neck blouse with a centre front/centre back opening.

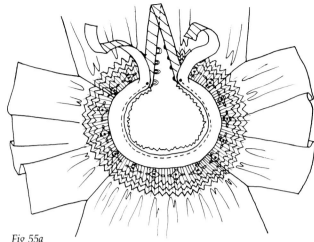

Fig 55a

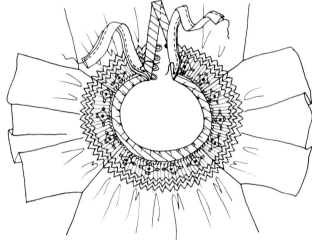

Fig 55b

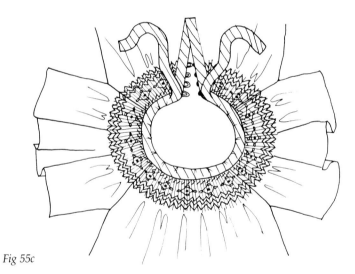

Fig 55c

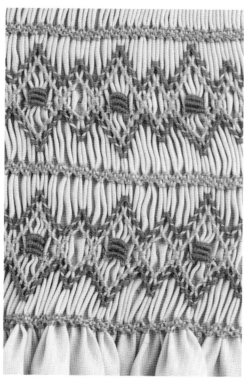

Right *Zainab in a sundress with a frill at the upper edge and Yumna in a sundress with binding at the upper edge*

Opposite *Kirsten in a waisted sundress and Michaela in a square necked sundress with a butterfly frill*

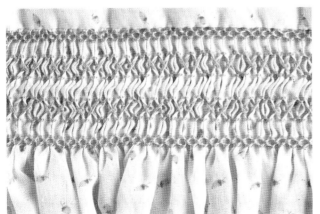

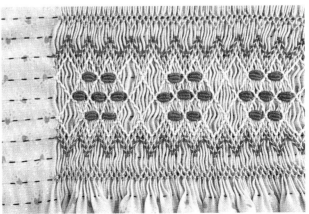

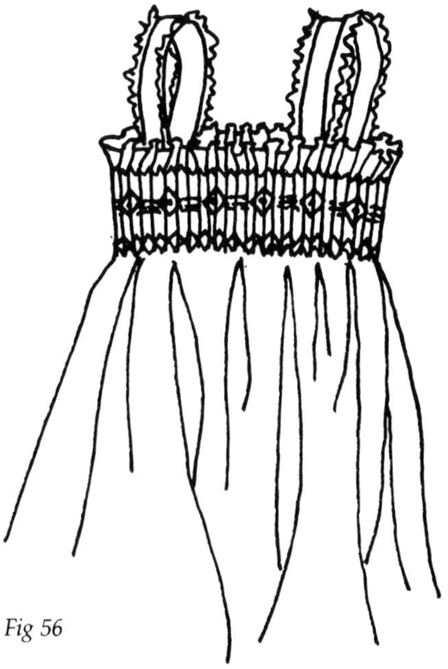

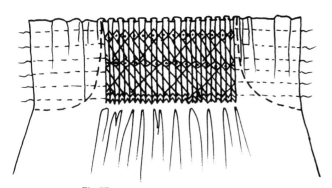

Fig 56

Sundresses

Sundresses, cool and practical for our hot summers, are extremely simple to make. A big advantage is that they do not restrict children's movement.

Straight sundress with frill at upper edge

Press the fabric to remove all creases and wrinkles. Check that the crosswise and lengthwise threads are at right angles to one another and cut off the selvages. Measure a 90 cm (36 inch) width of fabric for smocking the front and the same width for smocking the back. Cut two straps. Make a rolled hem across the top of the front and the back.

Depending on the age of the child, draw up between 7 and 16 gathering thread rows for smocking. Leave a 2 cm (¾ inch) frill at the top edge of the fabric or the raw edge if the top is to be bound. Leaving 5 pleats on either side of the fabric to allow for the seam, smock the design of your choice. Leave 6 pleats free of smocking at the centre back to allow for a seam or placket.

When your smocking is complete, pull out the gathering threads and block the completed smocking. Sew up side seams with right sides together and finish off the edges by machine with zigzag stitching. Cut down the back opening and make a placket opening or an open seam.

Fold straps in half lengthwise. With right sides together, stitch along the long edge and one end of the straps. Turn the straps to the right side and press. Stitch into position, slanting them towards the centre front and the centre back, to stop them slipping off the shoulders.

Sew on the buttons and make thread loops at the back. Hem the bottom edge of the completed sundress. (Fig 56)

Straight sundress with binding at upper edge

Stitch the side seams and complete the back as for the sundress with a frill. Cut a strip 3 cm (1¼ inches) longer than the chest measurement and 5 cm (2 inches) wide. Divide the strip into halves and quarters. With right sides together, pin the strip and frock together at centre front, under-arm and back of the bodice.

Stretch smocking to fit the strip and sew together. Trim the seam, fold over the strip and slipstitch into place on the wrong side.

Bound armhole sundress

Measure a 90 cm (36 inch) width of fabric for smocking the front and the same width for smocking the back. Make a rolled hem across the top of the front and back of the fabric. Prepare the fabric for smocking. Leaving 12 to 15 pleats on either side of the fabric to allow for the armhole, smock a design of your choice.

Fig 57a

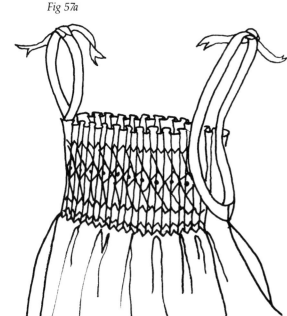

Fig 57b

After smocking, pull out the gathering threads and block the completed smocking. Place the regular commercial pattern piece on the smocking and cut out the armholes. Finish the armhole edge with bias binding cut from the same fabric as the dress and continue up for the strap. *(Fig 57a & b)*

Strip smocking

Smocking in strips that run from shoulders to waist is an interesting variation for a bodice you wish to smock over this area. This method takes far less time and uses less fabric than a fully smocked bodice. Obviously, the closeness of the strips to one another and their width will influence the amount of fabric required. As a guide, to calculate the width of fabric to be cut for smocking this type of bodice, measure the widest part of the bodice pattern piece, double this measurement if it is a 'whole' piece and quadruple it if it is a 'half' piece, i.e. a piece that would normally go on the fold.

Fig 58

A dress with a bodice smocked in strips should not require any more fabric than a conventional yoke dress. To calculate the length of fabric required, measure the person from shoulders to hemline, double this measurement and add the length of the sleeve.

Cut out a square or rectangular shape according to these measurements and gather up the required number of rows, using either the smocking pleater or dots. Tie off the gathering threads at each end of your prepared fabric, straighten the pleats and pull them out to measure approximately 3 cm to 5 cm (1¼ to 2 inches) shorter than the desired width. *(Fig 58)*

To minimize smocking in areas that will be cut away in the final construction of your garment, use the commercial pattern piece to mark out roughly any area on the prepared fabric that will be cut away after smocking is completed, i.e. neck and armhole curves. However, do not cut these areas until smocking has been completed.

Fig 59

Once completed, remove the gathering threads. To block the piece to the desired width, place the commercial pattern piece over the smocking and stretch to fit the pattern. Mark the smocked piece where it is to be cut. Stitch two rows of machine stitching – one on the marking and one just inside the first row. This will prevent the smocking from unravelling. *(Fig 59)*

Continue to make up the garment according to the instructions in the commercial pattern. Reinforce the seam that joins the smocked insert to the remainder of the garment with a double seam and zigzag stitching.

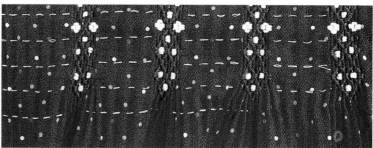

*Bronwen in a dress with a bodice
smocked in strips*

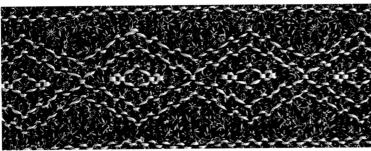

Lynne in a skirt smocked on the hips

Fig 60a

Waisted smocks

A waisted smock is smocked in front only and is a particularly good style for an older child who has outgrown the conventional yoke dress.

Do 6 to 8 rows of smocking on a piece of fabric 90 cm (36 inches) wide, that measures the waist to hem length plus the width of the area to be smocked. Using a commercial pattern with a bodice to the waist, cut out the back bodice according to the pattern. Cut out the front bodice shorter than the commercial pattern by the width of the area to be smocked, i.e. the smocked area of the skirt is inserted above the waistline. Make up the garment according to the directions accompanying your pattern and finish off with a tie belt or a tailor belt with buttons, attached in the side seams at the waist. (Fig 60a & b)

Fig 60b

Coats Anchor 8 metre stranded cottons used

Page	Name	Cottons	Page	Name	Cottons	Page	Name	Cottons	Page	Name	Cottons
6	Fiona	295	34	Lynne	386	56	Nicole	308	81	Kerry	167
		2						242			168
			35	Fiona	2			50			169
7	Ian	131						54			
		128	38	Jenny	22				84	Megan	36
		368				56	Alexandra	36			38
		295	38	Michaela	47			210			39
		46									
		214	39	Alasdair	47	60	Nicole	47	85	Michaela	25
		2	42	Emma	76			2			27
					268						
10	Julia and	46				61	Leigh-Anne	47	85	Ina	8
	Thomas	2						127			161
			43	Susan	75						
14	Samantha	372			268	64	Alexandra	47	88	Zainab	203
					42			2			50
15	Juliette	337									54
		13	46	Crib and	295	65	Sandra	47			
				Lampshade	298			127	88	Yumna	130
21	Helen	8									203
		10									24
		11	47	Robyn and	2	68	Nerine	117			
		212		Victoria	314			118	89	Kirsten and	2
					256			119		Michaela	52
24	Stitch	131									203
	Sampler	10				69	Ayesha	189			
			49	Stitch	131			118	92	Bronwen	133
25	Emma	131		Sampler	10						2
		128				72	Lynne and	47			
		2					Leigh-Anne	293	93	Lynne	2
			52	Alexandra	336			243			
28	Justin	186			337				96	Christmas	46
		187			339					Stocking	239
28	Lynne and	50				76	Leigh-Anne	133	96	Basket	303
	Leigh-Anne	54	53	Lynne and	337			131			
				Leigh-Anne	339			185	96	Cushion	386
29	Caroline	203			214			186			66
		117									165

95